THE PHILOSOPHY
OF DON HASDAI CRESCAS

COLUMBIA UNIVERSITY PRESS
SALES AGENTS

New York
LEMCKE & BUECHNER
30-32 East 20th Street

London.
HUMPHREY MILFORD
Amen Corner, E.C.

Shanghai
EDWARD EVANS & SONS, Ltd
30 North Szechuen Road

COLUMBIA UNIVERSITY ORIENTAL STUDIES

Vol. XVII

92

THE PHILOSOPHY
F DON HASDAI CRESCAS

BY

MEYER WAXMAN

Submitted in Partial Fulfilment of the Requirements
for the Degree of Doctor of Philosophy, in the
Faculty of Philosophy, Columbia University

New York
COLUMBIA UNIVERSITY PRESS
1920

55

A495422

PRINTED IN ENGLAND
AT THE OXFORD UNIVERSITY PRESS

NOTE

A PECULIAR interest attaches to Hasdaı Crescas. He swam against the current of the philosophical exposition of his day. He was bold enough to oppose the speculative reasoning of Aristotle, the man who held nearly all the philosophers ın his grip during so many centuıies, and, above all, he dared to crıticize the introductıon of Arıstotelıan views into the ıelıgious philosophy of hıs own people, even though these views were dıessed ın Jewısh garb by the master hand of Maimonides   The current passed him by, ıt could not overwhelm hım

In the following pages Dr Meyer Waxman has given us a detaıled and a very inteıestıng exposition of Creۭscas's philosophic system ; and he has added to thıs a comparison of Crescas's vıews, not only with those of Maimonides, but also wıth those of Spinoza.   We have thus lıned up foı us the three greatest mınds that speculative Jewish theology pıoduced duıing the Mıddle Ages, and the means are afforded us to estımate the value of theiı dip ınto the Unknown.

RICHARD GOTTHEIL

March 24, 1919.

TO MY WIFE

SARAH V. WAXMAN

PREFATORY NOTE

THE bulk of this study forming the body of the book, chapters i to vii inclusive, appeared originally in the *Jewish Quarterly Review*, New Series, Volumes VIII, Nos 3, 4, IX, Nos 1, 2, X, Nos 1, 2, 3.

To the editor and publishers of the Quarterly my thanks are due for their kindness in granting me the permission to reprint the articles in book form. The introductory chapter, dealing with the views held by the pre-Maimonidean philosophers on the problems discussed in Part I, was added for the purpose of supplying the reader with the necessary historical background. For the same reason it was deemed advisable to include in the introductory chapter a short account of Aristotle's theology, inasmuch as it forms the centre around which Jewish philosophic theology revolves

NEW YORK,
March 21, 1920.

BIOGRAPHICAL NOTE

Hasdai (or Chasdai) Crescas, the subject of this study, was born in Barcelona, Spain, in the year 1340. His family was one of the noblest and wealthiest among the Catalonian Jews, and supplied many a leader in communal affairs as well as in scholarship to Spanish Jewry Hasdai, despite his great Talmudic scholarship, never occupied any official Rabbinical position; his wealth made him completely independent. Yet the fact that he was a layman did not diminish his prestige. His fame spread far and wide throughout the diaspora, and his word was law to many Jewish communities Even the gentile world thought highly of him, for he stood in some degree of relationship to the court of James I of Aragon, and was often consulted on matters of state

Crescas's life, however, was not all bright, but had its dark shadows as well. As the result of a conspiracy, Crescas was accused before the court and was thrown into prison, together with some of the notables of Catalonian Jewry, among whom were some of his friends and also his teacher After a long term of imprisonment he was eventually released on bail. The persecution of 1391, which swept through Spain like a tornado, leaving behind desolation and ruin in most of the Jewish communities, failed not to include Crescas among its victims. In the massacre of Barcelona his only son was killed. Thereupon he removed to Saragossa, where the rest of his life was spent in philosophic study. He died in 1410

Besides his work *Or Adonai*, which contains his philo-sophico-theological speculations, Crescas wrote a polemical treatise against Christianity in which the fundamental doctrines of the church are analysed. The latter was written in Spanish and later translated into Hebrew. The *Or Adonai* was originally written in Hebrew.

TABLE OF CONTENTS

PART II. GOD AND THE WORLD

CHAPTER III

CHAPTER IV

CHAPTER V

CHAPTER VI

CHAPTER VII

THE PHILOSOPHY
OF DON HASDAI CRESCAS

INTRODUCTORY CHAPTER

I. General Characteristics of Jewish Philosophy.

JEWISH philosophy owes its birth to two great factors
that stimulated thought and intellectual pursuits in the
early mediaeval world in general, but more particularly
in the Arabic world of which the Jews formed a part.
These two factors were (1) the necessity arising among
theologians to defend their doctrines of faith from heresies[1]
which had their origin in the writings of the ancients,
portions of which were newly brought to light and widely
circulated during that period: (2) the rise of learning at
the dawn of the Middle Ages, which came as a reaction
against the ignorance that reigned in the preceding period
known as the Dark Ages.

Of these two factors, the latter preceded in point of
time, but the former was by far the more important. It is
a rather difficult task, however, to draw hard and fast lines
and fix the priority of one factor over another, for they
very often overlapped. The search for weapons of defence

---

[1] Cf Stöckler, *Geschichte der Philosophie des Mittelalters*, p 8

gave new impetus to the study of ancient writings. This, in turn, brought to light a multitude of new problems, which again opened up new fields for speculation. The apologetic tendency, however (though it never disappeared from mediaeval speculation), changed its form somewhat and expressed itself in a desire to rationalize religion—to found the principles of belief on a speculative basis. The famous maxim of Anselm, ' Credo ut intelligam ' is the formal expression of that striving [2] The purpose was not, as some think, to determine the nature of reason, and thus limit the field of philosophy, but, on the contrary, to set before the theologian a speculative end [3] This desire is manifest throughout mediaeval philosophic speculation, wherever it made its appearance, whether in the East or the West, and especially so in Jewish philosophy, where it assumed the leading motive, the apologetic tendency being relegated to the background.

The character of Jewish philosophy is thus already determined by the conditions of its birth as well as by the general trend of thought characteristic of that era   It retains conspicuously all the peculiarities of the age. It is receptive in content as well as in form. Authority predominates, personality and individual opinion fall to the background before a general abstract tone. The harmonistic or synthetic tendency to reconcile the conflicting opinions of various authorities holds a prominent place. Above all, it is theological and metaphysical.

As a result of its character, the problems with which Jewish philosophy concerns itself are limited. God occupies the central place around which the discussion turns. His

[2] Baeumker in *Allgemeine Geschichte der Philosophie*, p. 297.
[3] *Ibid.*

existence, the proofs of His essence, unity, and attributes are extensively discussed and commented upon. Next in importance to God is man, but this worthy object of thought is only viewed relatively, in the light of his relation to the Supreme Being. This situation gives rise to a discussion of human actions and involves the question of free will and determinism, Providence, and the problem of immortality. The latter includes the definition of the nature and essence of the soul, and presupposes a study of psychology in so far as it affects the nature and the position of the soul in the hierarchy of spiritual beings, and its participation in the activity of the intelligibles. A deeper insight into consciousness was unknown in that age. Logic occupied a worthy place as an instrumental means by which proofs were established and theories tested. The theory of knowledge was of little consequence in those days ; everything was revelation. Man was created for the purpose of knowing On the other hand, certain metaphysico-physical problems, such as time and space attracted great attention. Their importance lay in the fact that they were involved in the discussion of the proofs of the existence of God as well as in the question, all-important for theological purposes, of *creatio ex nihilo*. Inasmuch as in the treatment of these problems Jewish thinkers were greatly influenced by Arabic philosophy, and borrowed most of their material from it (in fact, Jewish philosophy can be said to be a child of the latter), a short survey of Arabic philosophy will help to make clear the degree of relationship between them and, at the same time, bring out the exact character of Jewish philosophy.

II. ARABIC PHILOSOPHY.

Arabic philosophy owes its birth to a combination of circumstances which made possible the continuation of Greek speculation in a modified form in the East after its exile from the West [4]   As Greek was hardly intelligible at this period in that part of the East, translations into Syriac, the vernacular, became a necessity   When the Arabs later conquered the country, learning received a fresh impetus.   New series of translations were undertaken from Syriac into Arabic, as well as from Greek into Arabic.[5]   The works translated were of a curious blend and included portions of Plato's Dialogues (especially Timaeus),[6] many of Aristotle's genuine works and many Pseudo-Aristotelian, Commentaries of Alexander of Aphrodisias, of Themistius, Porphyry's Isagoge, a few excerpts from the pre-Platonic philosophers, mostly of a pseudo character, and, finally, some of the Stoic works   The character of the works translated became an important factor in the development of Arabic philosophy.   The whole field of this philosophy was permeated with the spirit of Neo-Platonism, and even Aristotle's works were viewed through the same glasses   Because of this factor, the strain of Neo-Platonism was never removed from Arabic philosophy, and that, too, in its most Aristotelian period.   As a result of this, the centre of gravity in philosophic discussion shifted from purely Aristotelian problems to those which occupy an important place in the Neo-Platonic school such as the NOUS, the world-soul, &c.,

---

[4] In the time of Justinian, 529 A D

[5] De Boer, *History of Philosophy in Islam*, pp 15-17

[6] Stein, *C. G Ph*, p 323 and note 31.

which are rather of secondary consideration in Aristotle proper.[7]

Three tendencies are to be distinguished in the course of development of Arabic thought (a) the Calamitic, including its various forms such as the Mútakallimîn, the Mútazilites, and the Asherites; (b) the Neo-Platonic, and (c) the Aristotelian. The first is characterized by its predominant theological stamp and by its curious physical conceptions. Oddly enough, these theologians turned to Democritus rather than to Aristotle. They taught that things are composed of invisible atoms moving in the void and time is similarly composed of indivisible 'nows'. They combined this physical view with a queer theology. The atom is formless and attains perfection by receiving accidents which are momentarily created by God, and which alternately perish and are recreated. Some of the radical sects denied that there is continual creation, and declared the existence of stability in nature. The atomic theory was also applied to the soul. The soul was conceived to be a composition of fine atoms endowed with special accidents. They also held a peculiar view of reality. The senses are not reliable, and whatever is thinkable or even imaginable is possible, even if it be not in agreement with sensible reality.[8] The greatest objection to Aristotle was his contention as regards the eternity of the world, and because of this they turned to Democritus. The problem of the creation of the world occupied the most important place in their philosophic system and even became a means for proving the existence of God.

The second current of thought, the Neo-Platonic, found

---

[7] Stein, ibid.

[8] Maimonides, *Guide of the Perplexed*, vol. i, ch 73

its exponents in the Society of the Brothers, who flourished in the Tenth Century and left behind a cyclopedia in which their ideas are preserved. This line of thought, as its origin testifies, is mystical in character. The theory of emanation, the development of the soul through lower forms into the human, its return to its source after purification by means of the knowledge of truth, are some of its teachings.[9]

The third tendency in Arabic philosophy, the Aristotelian, is the most important. Its chief exponents, Al-Kindi (870), Al-Farabi, Ibn Sina (1037), and Ibn Roshd (1198), have attained renown. However, even here, Neo-Platonism is not banished; Al-Farabi still teaches it, the NOUS $\pi o\iota\eta\tau\iota\kappa\delta s$—another name for the world-soul—is all-important. Another doctrine of great value was the Averroistic 'unitas intellectus', which taught that there is no individual intellect but rather a universal one, the active reason, and it is individual only in so far as any one personal mind participates in the general. The question of the eternity of the world was another difficult and keenly perplexing problem which Averroes was finally compelled to admit and as a result, to limit creation to the forms.[10]

All these movements, currents, and undercurrents of thought agitating the Arabic world have their counterpart in Jewish philosophy, which may also be divided into three similar periods in which the above-mentioned tendencies prevailed, viz. (a) the Mutakallimin, of which many Karaite writers and principally the Rabbinist Saadia (940) are the exponents; (b) the Neo-Platonic, represented by Ibn Gabirol and partly by Bahya; and (c) the Aristotelian, whose

---

[9] Goldziher in *Allgemeine Geschichte der Philosophie*, p 53
[10] Goldziher, 58-64

spokesmen are Abraham Ibn Daud, Maimonides, and Gersonides. Crescas stands apart from all these and resembles more closely the Arabic philosopher Al-Gazali, who, in his book *Destructio Philosophorum,* likewise attacked the philosophic doctrines of his age and attempted to show their fallibility. These divisions, however, are to be regarded as rough landmarks rather than as fixed boundaries. Jewish philosophy is not entirely a shadow of Arabic philosophy. It can lay claim to individuality and initiative. Its exponents never followed blindly any one Arabic school, but rather chose various theories from each school, especially those that stood a rigid test of criticism.

III   HISTORICAL SURVEY OF THE TREATMENT OF THE PROBLEMS RELATIVE TO THE EXISTENCE OF GOD AND HIS ATTRIBUTES BY THE CHIEF JEWISH PHILOSOPHERS

Saadia (892–942), the first Rabbinic philosopher, followed the indirect method of the Mutakallimîn in his philosophic proofs of the existence of God. To them, the question of *creatio ex nihilo* was an all-important one, and to it they devoted all their energies. The existence of God was a necessary corollary to this question , for, granted that the world is created, the existence of a creator must be posited. Saadia, however, followed the Mutakallimîn more in method than in content. Of his eight proofs only a few agree with those of the Mutakallimîn as quoted by Maimonides. The proofs for the existence of God are arranged by Saadia in the following order .

I. The world is finite—a fact, demonstrated according to the knowledge of his times. This is also one of the fundamental principles of Aristotle. Again, a finite body must necessarily possess a finite moving power (this is likewise one of Aristotle's propositions and was used repeatedly in his proofs of the existence of God). Like every finite thing, the world, therefore, must have a beginning, and hence was created. The corollary of the existence of a creator is more implied than expressed. The proof, however, is not absolutely convincing ; for, one may argue, granted that the world has a beginning, it still may not have a creator. It may have arisen by chance Saadia himself argues later against the theory of chance.

II. The world-matter is composite and, as every composed thing, it is possible of existence, for the elements *per se* have no natural tendency to stay apart or to be united If such a tendency existed, either the elements would stay apart for ever or would never decompose. The case, however, is not so. It follows, therefore, that there must be some external source affecting their composition, and as cause follows cause, there is of necessity some final creator. This last agrees with the third proof used by the Mutakallimîn as quoted by Maimonides (*Guide of the Perplexed*, I, 74). It is also similar to the cosmological proof formulated by Leibnitz, although somewhat differently expressed.

III. We observe in the world of things that accidents are continually generated and destroyed But accidents are inseparably inherent in substance ; it, therefore, follows that if accidents have a beginning matter must have as well, and hence must have a creator. This proof agrees entirely with the fourth of the Mutakillimîn cited by Maimonides, and is directly connected with the Calamitic theoly of mattei which assumes [11] that the atom becomes matter only through its accidents. But this is untenable according to the Aristotelian notion of primal matter, which is said to be a substance devoid of accidents and is known as ether.

IV. Time must be finite. For, assuming that time is infinite and, as is usual, is conveniently divided into past, present, and future, the present ' now ' which has no magnitude may, for the sake of argument, be taken as a starting-point If we then tiy in our imagination to ieach upward from that point, the human reason is unable to grasp the fact that time is infinite This being the case, how could existence ever reach us, since an infinity never ends ? We, however, do exist. It follows, therefore, that time is finite ; and accordingly the world which is in time had a beginning and a creatoi. This proof is Calamitic in form, especially the emphasis laid upon unthinkability of the infinite with a view to its unreality —Aristotle produces a similar argument as regards the infinite.—The dictum that whatever is unthinkable is also non-existent was a fundamental principle with this school The pioof itself, howevei, survived long in philosophic literature, and is repeated by Kant in his thesis of the first antinomy, wheie almost the exact aigument is ieproduced with the omission of the part played by unthinkability.

Saadia brings forth thiee more proofs of a direct character. (1) Things could not create themselves. It is evident that the state of being is more peifect than that of becoming. But we see that if in the state of being a thing happens to be imperfect it cannot become more

[11] See above, section 2

perfect by its own means, but needs the help of an external agent; how then could it become at all by itself? [12]   A similar argument is quoted by Albertus Magnus. (2) It is impossible for things to create themselves on account of the peculiar nature of time.   Time is only conventionally divided into three parts, while in reality there are only two; for, the present has no duration.   The question thereupon arises when could things create themselves?   In the time previous to their origin they were not in existence; then how could a non-existing thing create itself?   And to say that they created themselves after their coming into existence is highly absurd.   To speak of their creating themselves at the particular moment of coming into existence is meaningless, for that moment of time cannot be isolated since it is a 'now' and therefore has no duration. (3) If we endow things with the ability to create themselves, we must also concede them the power of not entering into existence, for otherwise things would always exist   We posit then two contraries at one and the same time.   In order to fortify himself against every form of attack, Saadia reproduces the famous Aristotelian proposition which demonstrates the impossibility of an infinite causal series.[13]   He employs it, however, to disprove the eternity of matter and not to prove that there is a final moving cause, as the philosophers do.   By this he wishes to imply that material causes could not go on infinitely but must have had a beginning.

After the proofs for the existence of God had been

[12] Fürst's interpretation of this passage has been used   It is true that the passage lends itself to a more strict interpretation, but for philosophical clearness of thought a full interpretation seems more advisable.

[13] *Metaphysics*, a 2.

satisfactorily disposed of, Saadia proceeds to prove that there is only one God. He brings forward the following arguments. (1) Since it was proved that God is the cause of all being, it follows that he is incorporeal; for every form of being is composite, and a composite thing cannot be an ultimate cause, since it needs some other external cause to effect its composition. Were there more gods than one, the conception of God would fall under the category of number, and whatever is in the category of number is corporeal. It is evident, therefore, that God is one.[14] (2) There cannot be two gods; for, if there were two, we must assume that in the act of creation they cannot act independently but need mutual help. In such case they are determined and one is the cause of the other—an assumption directly in contradiction to the conception of God as the sole ultimate cause. On the other hand, should we assume their absolute independence, the act of creation is hardly conceivable; for a conflict would of necessity ensue.[15] The strength of this proof is best comprehended on comparing it with the fifth proof of the Mutakallimîn as quoted by Maimonides,[16] where the reasoning is improved in logical strength by the supply of a link in the chain of argument, viz. ' If, on assuming that the two gods are independent, we must also assume that each one is potent enough to create the world, then the other is entirely superfluous.' (3) The third proof is very logical, and is the strongest. How shall we conceive these two gods? Are they exactly alike in substance without the least difference? If so, they are one and not two. Wherefore,

---

[14] Cf. Maimonides, *Guide* Proposition 16 quoted from Aristotle.

[15] Cf. *infra*, Chapter I, and the objection of Crescas to such proof

[16] G. P., Ch 75. Cf D. Kaufmann, *Attributenlehre*

we must assume that they are different, but not entirely different, they must be similar at least in as far as both are gods. Each one of them will accordingly have points of difference and points of similarity, and will as a result, be composite—a fact contrary to the conception of God.

The fact that to Saadia the creation of the world is an all-important principle affected his theory of attributes. He derives them solely from the concept creator. They are very few in number, living, potent, and wise. Willing is left out, for it is not strictly inherent in the concept creator. It implies the notion of striving to an end and so necessarily involves a limitation.[17] Besides, potent really includes willing[18] These attributes do not imply any change in his essence, they denote really one thing. The attributes are not separated from his being but exist through his being. In God, existence and essence are one. God is beyond any categories, even that of quality. The emotional qualities often ascribed to Him, such as loving or hating, are to be understood in a rather figurative way. God commanded certain precepts and those who follow them are said to be loved, on the contrary those who disobey them are described as being hated[19] When speaking of God as being an agent, we must conceive it in a different sense than the agency of man, for contrary to man He is not moved while acting and is always active.[20] The many adjectives of God which are often mentioned in the Bible, whether emotional or active, are all relative, describing His relation in reference to His creatures.

---

[17] Cf Spinoza Appendix to v 1, Ethics.

[18] Kaufmann, *Attributenlehre* p 27, N. 54.

[19] *Emunoth ve Deoth*, ed Kitower, *Jusefof*, 1885, p 50 a.

[20] *Ibid*, p 51 a.

Saadia really laid the philosophic basis of the theory of attributes. His followers improved upon the form of the theory, but hardly added anything to the contents.

Bahya, the next representative Jewish philosopher after Saadia, is a little less complicated in his proofs, but bears such a resemblance to Saadia, that to quote his proofs in full would be mere repetition. He, like Saadia, employs the indirect method in establishing the existence of God, namely, by proving that this world has a creator. Bahya posits three principles (1) A thing does not create itself. (2) The series of beings is finite, and as such had a beginning. (3) Every composite thing is generated. He proves the first in exactly the same way as Saadia did,[21] showing the impossibility of locating the moment of self-creation, but fails to mention the division of time which really forms the basis of the proof. The second is proved through the demonstration of the finitude of time employed by Saadia, and supported by the famous Aristotelian argument against the infinite of 'the part and the whole'.[22] The third is proved by observation. These physical proofs are fortified by a beautiful exposition of the argument from design

It is rather curious that the argument from design, which is frequently mentioned in Rabbinic literature (cf. Bereshit Rabba, Chapter 39) and even hinted at in the Bible (cf. Ps. 8) should be so little employed in Jewish philosophy It is only in Bahya and Halevi that we find it mentioned. It is probably because these two pay more attention to the ethical side of religion than to the dogmatic theological

Bahya's proofs of unity are interesting. Some of them are reproductions of the proofs offered by Saadia, but some

[21] Cf above, p. 10.
[22] Cf. ch 1, p 38

are original. He adduces seven proofs of which the third,
fourth, and seventh agree with the second, third, and fourth
of Saadia. The others are stated in the following manner
(1) In observing the world of things, we notice an ascending
scale of causes   Their number is always less than that
of the things caused,[23] and the higher we ascend in the
scale of being, the fewer the causes become. It follows,
then, that on reaching the top of the ladder, there must be
only one cause. (2) Design testifies not only to a creator
but also to one, for the world is so beautifully harmonious
that we must involuntarily conclude that it is the plan of
one creator. (3) One is the fundamental basis of number
and measure.   Before there is plurality there must be
unity, for plural means only so many times one. It is
evident, therefore, that there must be only one ultimate
cause, for if we agree that there is more than one creator,
there must by necessity be one preceding, and then he is
the God. (4) Plurality must have accidents, for it is sub-
sumed under the category of quantity, and this is contrary
to the conception of God.   This last proof is analogous to
Saadia's first proof, but expressed in a different form.

In the theory of attributes, Bahya diverges greatly from
Saadia in naming such attributes as are entirely omitted
by the former.   The difference arises through the variance
of the method of derivation   Bahya divides the attributes
into two classes, essential and active. Saadia also uses the
same names indirectly for various classes of attributes, but
the name essential has a different meaning with Saadia.
Saadia viewed the attributes *sub specie creationis*, since they
are all derived from the notion creator. Bahya, on the

---

[23] e g the genera are less than the species, the categories less than the
genera.

other hand, views them *sub specie speculationis*, and they
are, therefore, according to him, existent, one, and eternal,
such as have been proven to belong to God by philosophical
demonstration. That these attributes are sublime, pure,
and abstract in character, and approach the highest philosophic conception of God, is self-evident. The term essential, by which Bahya describes the foregoing attributes,
signifies that these attributes are to be predicated of God
independently of the fact that he is the creator of the
world. These attributes, though in relation to God are
named essential, yet, as far as the human mind is concerned, express only a negative meaning. The second
class, the active, describe the relations of God to the world
and men through actions They are of course figurative in
sense, and resorted to only by force of necessity.[24]

Jehuda Halevi (1140) is more of an ethical philosopher
than a metaphysical one His book, the *Kuzari*, is so
religiously inspired that it can hardly be expected of its
author to endeavour to prove the existence of God, when
such a thing is self-evident. The fact that all humanity
believes in the existence of God is sufficient for him. This
kind of proof is indirectly inferred from the whole tenor of
the book, and especially from the fact that in his arguments
about the truth of the Jewish tradition he lays great
emphasis upon the *consensus omnium*.[25] He makes also
occasional and indirect mention of the argument from
design.[26]

His theory of attributes, however, is quite interesting

---

[24] Passages used in exposition of Bahya's doctrine are found in *Hobot ha-Lebbabot*, ed Wilna Tractat, 1, pp 66–92

[25] The same proof was extensively used among the Christian Philosophers

[26] *Kuzari*, ed. Isaac Metz, II, p 27

for its method of division. Halevi divides the attributes
into three kinds : active, relative, and negative. The active
are derived through the description of God's actions, and
include the emotional. The relative are such that men
bestow upon Him, as praised, holy, sublime, &c   They
are, therefore, entirely subjective, and are related to the
human state of mind   The most important attributes,
the essential as Bahya would call them, are the negative.
They are living, one, and first and last. These connote
nothing else but the denial of the opposite. In reality, we
hardly conceive the kind of life we attribute to God, and
it is surely absolutely different from our conception of life,
but we express it in the positive form in order to ward off
the popular conception that he who is not alive is dead.
The same is to be said about the rest. It is to be noticed
that although Bahya mentions that his essential attributes
have a negative meaning, he does not name them negative ,
and, on the contrary, his naming shows that they really
have positive contents. Halevi was the first philosopher
who introduced the term negative (in Rabbinic), and used
it in accordance with its logical meaning. He also names
will an attribute, a thing which his predecessors avoided
and which philosophy always shrank from. He uses as his
defence the argument from design which shows that not
only is there a creator but also a wilful one.[27]

Abraham Ibn Daud (died 1160), the last of the Jewish
philosophers of the Pre-Maimonidian period, shows himself
a follower of Aristotle, and accordingly his arguments and
proofs are more philosophic in contents as well as in form.
Of the proofs for the existence of God, he adduces two,
which are really one under two forms. The first is the

[27] *Kusari*, ed Isaac Metz, II, p. 27.

famous Aristotelian used over and over, and even mentioned by Saadia and Bahya, but never as yet produced in its pure philosophic form till Ibn Daud. It runs as follows. There is no infinite body, there is also no infinite power in a finite body, but the first sphere moves eternally, there must, therefore, be a prime mover. This prime mover is incorporeal, for since it does not move itself it is not in time. (The premisses, as well as the conclusions, of this proof will be discussed in full later.) If it is not in time, it is infinite; again, since it is infinite it is not body, for body is finite.[28] The second proof is analogous to one mentioned by Saadia, but it is expressed in better logical form, and therefore more convincing. The world of things presents to us continual possibility. There must be one thing necessary of existence, for the possible of existence requires a cause, and so we would have an infinite causal regressus, but that is impossible. Out of the fundamental conception of God being necessary of existence, Ibn Daud deduces the unity of God The fact that God is necessary of existence implies that He is absolutely simple, for every composite thing is possible This, however, proves simplicity. As for the numerical unity, he adduces the famous Saadianic-Bahyan arguments of the impossibility of the existence of two Gods. Unity, according to him, belongs to the essence of God, and has therefore a negative ring.

His theory of attributes shows rather a concession to popular demand than to philosophy. He enumerates the largest number of attributes ever stated by a Jewish philosopher. There are eight attributes according to him, they are, one, existent, true, eternal, living, knowing, willing, and potent. He could not help but realize that

[28] Cf. with this conclusion that of Aristotle in *Metaphysics*, book K x

W.   C

there are several superfluities in his list. Let us take the attribute, living, since we continue counting knowing, willing, it is already evident that God is living. But, says Ibn Daud in his defence, when speaking of attributes, we should not leave too much to logical reasoning, but rather be popular. Truthful is an interesting attribute Ibn Daud is the only one that employs it. It is according to him connected with existent. What do we mean by truth and error, except the real and the unreal, says Ibn Daud [29] God is always real, therefore he is the source of truth. Yet in spite of the fact that Ibn Daud is not very accurate in his enumeration of the attributes, he is as zealous in his interpretation of them as any other philosopher to remove even a probable shadow of corporeality from God He, therefore, insists that whatever the attributes express *per se*, to us they have only a negative meaning.[30]

IV. THE THEOLOGY OF ARISTOTLE.

In order to elucidate the philosophical ground of the theology of the Jewish philosophers, the Pre-Maimonidean, as well as Maimonides, and the Post-Maimonidean, including Crescas, a brief outline of Aristotle's theological view is necessary. Aristotle proves the existence of a first cause in several ways ; though they may be ultimately reduced to one, yet differ in form. In the *Metaphysics*, Aristotle proves the existence of God in the following manner There must exist an eternal immovable substance. It must be eternal, for since substance is the first of existing things, it must be indestructible, in order that things should not all be destructible. Again, movement is eternal, for

[29] Cf. P W. Montague in his essay 'Truth and Error', *New Realism*
[30] *Eimuna Romah*, Exalted Faith, ed Wilna, p. 51-6.

time is, and movement is connected with it. That which is causing movement must be something necessary of existence, for it is constantly active, and if the cause were not necessary of existence, movement would not be eternal. The first heaven is eternally moved, but everything which is moved must have a mover. There is, therefore, an eternal mover. This mover is unmoved, for a thing that moves and is moved is only a secondary, never a first cause, and since there must be a first cause for there is no infinite causal regressus, the first mover is immovable.[31] In the *Physics*,[32] the same proof from motion is produced but more emphasis is laid on the non-existence of an infinite, and the impossibility of an infinite causal regressus. The metaphysical argument that there must be one necessary cause in this world, for all possible is only potential, but not constantly active,—its ground is really the supposition that there cannot be any infinite causal series,—was very often used by early scholastic philosophers as well as by Pre-Maimonidean Jewish philosophers in various modified forms, though the basal proposition was frequently omitted. Again, in the *Fragments*,[33] Aristotle proves the existence of God by the arrangement of the series of beings in the world order. We note that there is a variety of beings, and that this variety is arranged in an ascending scale, there must be then one being who is the highest in that ascending series, or, to express it differently, the last link in that chain. This proof was also utilized by various Christian and Jewish philosophers.[34]

As regards the attributes of that first cause, or God,

---

[31] *Metaphysics*, XII, C. 6-7.
[32] *Physics*, VIII, C. 8-10.   [33] *Fragments*, 15.
[34] Cf above, section III, in the exposition of Bahya's views.

they follow mostly from the nature of the proofs. God exists, and his existence is necessary, as has been shown, and not only necessary but eternal. All this follows directly from the conception of a first mover. Further, since God is necessary, He is also excellent or good;[35] for the necessary, without which things cannot be, is also good by its own definition.[36] Life is also an attribute of God, for according to the Aristotelian conception the highest activity is thought, and the actuality of thought is life, and since God possesses the highest activity, it follows that He possesses life. Moreover, that life is a beatific one   This follows from the same conception, since the best enjoyments that we humans have in life are those of mental activities; God, whose activity *eo ipso* is thought, must necessarily be happy. God is also without any magnitude, for He cannot be a finite magnitude, since He produces motion in infinite time, and no finite body can possess an infinite power.[37] Again, He cannot be of infinite magnitude, since there are no such magnitudes. He must, therefore, be without any parts and indivisible   There is only one first cause, for there is only one heaven   Would there be many, there would be several movers who would be one in principle and several in number. This supposition would imply the materiality of the Gods, for that which imparts individuality to a member of a species is the matter since the form is one; but we proved that the first cause is incorporeal and therefore one.[38]

The foregoing proved the existence of a God and endeavoured to describe, though abstractly, His nature and essence. The question still remains, and a very important

---

[35] *Metaphysics*, XII, 7   [36] *Ibid*
[37] *Ibid.*, XII, 7, *Physics*, VIII   [38] *Ibid*, XII, C. 8.

one, what is the relation of this God to the world of which
He is the first cause and principle? This is a very difficult
problem, and was left rather unexplained by Aristotle.
The essential activity of God is thought, but what is the
nature of His thought? To this Aristotle answers explicitly,
that since the thoughts must be of the best kind, the object
of His thinking is He himself.[39] Such an answer made the
question more difficult, for if all that He does is to think of
Himself, how is He to be considered a first cause of the
world? True, the first of Aristotle must be understood not
as first in time, since movement is eternal, and, therefore,
contemporaneous with the mover, but a kind of logical
priority;[40] but still how is the causality effected? Aristotle
explains that He moves the spheres by desire. There is
a kind of Divine love which prompts the beings to seek
Him. However, it does not remove the difficulty, for this
desire is located in the world and not in Him, and the
question how this world with its multiple changes and
striking order came about, and how and why that desire
exists, is still an open one. The God of Aristotle is not an
efficient cause, and exercises no influence upon the world of
which He is supposed to be the principle. It is true,
Aristotle sees a unity in nature, and even quotes the line
from Homer, 'The rule of many is not good, one is the
ruler'.[41] But how is his 'One', as conceived by him, the
ruler? The later philosophers, especially the disciples of
the Alexandrian school, saw in Aristotle's God an efficient
cause and attributed to him providence.[42] A number of

[39] *Ibid*, XII, 9.

[40] Cf Caird, *Evolution of Theology in Greek Thought*, V, II, p 15.

[41] *Metaphysics*, XII, 10.

[42] Quoted by Jules Simon in *Étude sur la Théodicée de Platon et d'Aristote*, p 90.

mediaeval theologians assumed the same view, among them Thomas Aquinas.[43] They tried to overcome the difficulty by positing that the thoughts of God include a kind of ideal principles or intelligibles which are realized in the world. Thomas Aquinas says, 'Since God is the cause of things the effects are contained in Him, and thus it follows that God in knowing Himself knows the world.[44] To this Jules Simon[44] rightly objects that St. Thomas confounds the conception of a cause with a logical priority, for God, as understood by Aristotle, is only the latter and not a preceding cause. A similar conclusion to that of Thomas is reached also by Caird in his quoted work. However, the whole conception of the realization of ideal principles is entirely extraneous to the Aristotelian philosophy and it is rather Platonic.

It is evident that such a theology, no matter how scientific it might have been, could hardly be accepted by men to whom religion was not a mere matter of speculation, but of tradition and dogma, to whom God was not only a logical principle but an active force in life. It had to be modified by them and opposed in part. It elucidated the fact why most of the Pre-Maimonidean Jewish philosophers insisted so strenuously on the creation of the world, and why they endeavoured to prove it before the existence of God They felt that unless God is proved to be an active creative force, His existence is valueless for religious purposes. It is only in Maimonides, who followed Aristotle closely, that creation loses its force. It also illustrates to a certain degree the opposition of Crescas to Maimonides

[43] l.c, p. 100

[44] 'Patet quod Deus cognoscendo se ipsum omnia cognoscit opera', p. 462

PART I

GOD

NOTE ON CRESCAS'S PHILOSOPHICAL POSITION

WITH Hasdai Crescas, the list of Jewish mediaeval thinkers, worthy of the name, closes; but his importance lies rather in his own originality than in his chronological position. He is among the few Jewish philosophers who exhibited originality of thought, critical acumen, and logical sequence, combined with a profound religious feeling. It is rather the irony of fate that this philosopher, who surpasses in depth and power of analysis even Maimonides, should have received rather slight attention at the hands of the historians of Jewish thought. The books and articles dealing with Crescas are few in number The book by M. Joel, *Chasdai Crescas*, is perhaps the largest and best of them, but, with all its merits, it fails to present a comprehensive view of Crescas's thought. It is therefore the hope of the present writer that the attempt in the following pages to present a systematic treatment of the philosophical conceptions of Crescas will be welcomed by students of the history of Jewish thought in particular, and of philosophy in general.

The method adopted in treating the subject is the problematic one; chiefly because it is the most elucidating in dealing with a subject of a philosophico-theological character such as ours, and also because the work of Crescas, *Or Adonai*, 'The Light of God,' lends itself to such treatment, since it is primarily a book on dogmatics and follows the usual division into dogmas. As the main interest of this study lies in the philosophic aspect of Crescas's thinking, only such problems have been included as have a philosophic bearing, while all purely theological questions have been excluded. For this reason, all detailed discussion concerning *creatio ex nihilo*, wherein Crescas opposes Gersonides with great critical ability, are omitted. Broadly speaking, the study is divided into two parts corresponding to the two central ideas around which the problems group themselves, viz. (*a*) God, (*b*) God and the world—the problems themselves being treated in the various chapters and subdivisions.

The theses laid down in this study are the following ·

§ 1. Crescas holds a prominent place as a critical examiner of some of the important Aristotelian conceptions such as space, time, and the infinite. His criticism is decidedly modern in spirit, and some of his anticipations and theories were later fully corroborated by the founders of modern philosophy and cosmology. These anticipations, together with his revolt against Aristotelianism in an age when it was all-dominating, prove the high character of his work Moreover, his thoughts on this subject were not entirely restricted to a small circle of readers of Hebrew, but also found their way to the external world. It follows, therefore, that the seeds sown by Crescas are not only valuable in themselves, but have borne fruit, though how this was accomplished is not known. It is extremely difficult to trace the path over which thought travels.

§ 2. The study intends to point out the mental proximity between Crescas and that great Jewish thinker Spinoza. An attempt has been made to draw a sketch of Crescas's positive philosophy, which has been compared at each step

with that of Spinoza's system. Great care was observed
in avoiding final decisions in regard to the influence of the
former upon the latter. Unfortunately, the term influence
is often misunderstood to mean either a direct borrowing
or at least a kind of imitation If influence is to be
interpreted in a broad sense, and is to imply the existence
of a number of points of contact, and the supply of a certain
motive power or impulse in a definite direction by one
system upon another, such an influence of Crescas upon
Spinoza probably exists The word *probably* is used
advisedly, for the evidence at hand only justifies us in
using the term influence with this qualification

Crescas, however, is only an indirect critic of Aristotle
through his attack on Maimonides' proof of the existence
of God and theory of attributes which embody the
Aristotelian principles. Hence it is that in order to
elucidate Crescas's contribution to Jewish and general
philosophy we have to turn to Maimonides first.
Maimonides collected twenty-six propositions, which are
found scattered through the *Physics*, *Metaphysics*, and
De Caelo, and on these as a basis he reared his philosophical theology. Crescas reproduces these propositions
in full, and even quotes at length their proofs which were
omitted by Maimonides, and then launches his criticism
not only against Maimonides but against Aristotle himself
It was rather a bold attempt for those times (end of the
fourteenth century) to dare to criticize Aristotle, but he
pursued it with unflinching persistency. It is necessary,
in order to have a full comprehension of Don Hasdai's
philosophy, to follow him in all the intricate mazes of
Aristotelian physics. We will, therefore, quote the propositions verbatim.

CHAPTER I

MAIMONIDES' PROOFS OF THE EXISTENCE OF GOD. CRITICISM AND OBJECTION OF CRESCAS.

I. Infinite magnitude does not exist.[1] This proposition is a fourfold one, and the most important of all. It will be discussed in its four aspects, together with the proofs and Crescas's objections   II The simultaneous existence of an infinite number of bodies of finite magnitude is impossible [2] This proposition is simply a corollary of the first, for if the existence of such a number of bodies would be possible, the sum of all would give us an infinite magnitude, and this has been proved unreal   III. There is no infinite causal regressus, that is, the series of causes that lead up to the present world of things is not infinite, but must have had a beginning.[3]   IV. Change is found in four categories, that of substance, quantity, quality, and that of place , corresponding respectively to the categories, we have generation and corruption ($\gamma\acute{\epsilon}\nu\epsilon\sigma\iota\varsigma$ $\kappa\alpha\grave{\iota}$ $\phi\theta o\rho\acute{\alpha}$), growth and decay, qualitative change, and locomotion or spatial.[4]   V. Motion is a change from the potential to the actual.[5] VI. Movement

[1] שמציאות בעל שעור אחד אין תכלית לו שקר, *Moreh Nebukim*, Wilna, 1904 II, first hakdamah, *Guide of the Perplexed*, Eng tr by Friedlander, Part II, 1 ; *Physics*, III, 5, 7, ed Prantl, Greek and German, Leipzig, 1854, *Metaph* , XI, 10

[2] *Guide, ibid.*, p 2; *Physics, ibid*

[3] שמציאות עלות ועלולים אין תכלית למספרם שקר והמשל בו שיהיה השכל הזה על דרך משל סבתו שכל שני, וסבת השני שלישי, וסבת השלישי רביעי כן אל לא תכלית, זה גם בן שקר מבואר, *Guide, ibid* ; *Metaph*, II

[4] *Guide, ibid., Physics,* III, 1 , *Metaph* XII, 2

[5] *Physics*, III, 1 ; *Metaph* XI, 9

is of four kinds, essential, accidental, forced, and partial.[6] Essential movement means the movement of a body according to its nature and essence. Accidental pertains to the movement of an accident, such as the movement of blackness in a body from one place to another, blackness being only an accident. By the partial is meant the movement of a part of a body when the whole is moved, but with reference to that part, such as the movement of a nail in a ship, which is moved by the movement of the ship as a whole Partial movement, as different from accidental, refers to such things as are bodies for themselves, but are attached by artificial means to another body.   Forced movement includes all kinds of movement which are unnatural. According to Aristotle, each of the elements has a natural place whither it tends.   A movement in that direction is natural ; thus the natural movement of fire is upwards and of earth downwards , but a movement in the opposite direction is unnatural.   The movement of a stone upwards is contrary to nature, and can be accomplished only by the force exerted by the thrower. VII. Whatever changes is divisible, and whatever is not divisible does not move and is no body.[7] Aristotle proves this by explaining that every change is an intermediary state between two opposites,[8] or between a *terminus a quo* and a *terminus ad quem* , therefore, a body in the state of change must necessarily be divisible, and since movement is a kind of change, it follows that whatever is moved is divisible, and also the converse.   VIII. Whatever moves

---

מו"ג .התנועות מהן בעצם מהן במקרה ומהן בהכרח ומהן בחלק [6] חלק ב' /, *Moreh*, II, 3 , *Physics*, VIII, 4.

[7] Τò δὲ μεταβάλλον ἄπαν ἀνάγκη διαιρετὸν εἶναι, *Physics*, VI, 4.

[8] *Metaph.* 1069 b.

accidentally will ultimately rest of necessity.[9] This is based
on Aristotle's conception of the accidental which identifies
it with the possible. Whatever is possible must of necessity
become actual in infinite time. Every possible has two
phases, e. g. possible of existence, it is possible for it to
exist, and possible not to exist. Both of these two possibilities must be realized in an infinite time, for if not, the
thing is either necessarily existing or necessarily non-
existing. Likewise, the possible of movement when it does
move will ultimately rest, for the opposite must necessarily
be realized. IX. A body moving another body is itself
moved at the same time.[10] This, however, does not include
such things as move others by being an end to which things
strive. It was on account of this fact that Aristotle made
the unmoved mover the end of existence, for otherwise
he could not be a first cause. The mediaeval philosophers,
however, had some difficulty with this proposition. The
magnet attracting iron and moving it towards itself seemed
to form an exception to the rule laid down in the proposition.[11] Various answers were given but are too absurd to
reproduce. X. Whatever pertains to body, either the body
is the stay of it, e. g. accidents, or it is the stay of the body,
as form.[12] XI. Some things that have their stay in the
body are divided when the body is divided, as accidents
are. Some things that are the stay of the body, e. g soul,
are not divided.[13] XII Every force pertaining to body is

---

[9] *Physics*, V, 3   [10] *Ibid.*, VIII, 5

[11] וכבר הקשי על זה ממה שנראה בחוש שהאבן המגניטס שיניע הברזל
כשימשכהו אצלו ולא יתנועע, *Or Adonai*, ed Vienna, p 9 b.

[12] אם שתהיה עמידתו בנשם במקרים, או שתהיה עמידת הנשם בו בצורה
הטבעית, *Moreh*, II, 5 ; *Physics*, VIII, 10.

[13] *Ibid*

finite, since body is finite [14]   XIII. All kinds of changes
are not continuous, except spatial motion, and of it only the
circular [15]   XIV. Spatial motion is the first of movements
both in nature and in time.[16]   XV. Time is an accident of
motion, and both are so related that they exist simultaneously   There is no movement but in time, and whatever
has no movement is not in time [17]   XVI. Whatever is not
a body does not fall under the category of number.[18]
XVII Whatever is moved has a mover, either as an
external force or as an internal tendency which is the cause
of the movement [19]   XVIII. Whatever is being realized
in passing from the potential to the actual, the cause of
the realization is external by necessity.[20]   It could not be
inherent in the thing itself, for in that case the thing would
never be possible, but always existing.   XIX. Whatever
has a cause for its existence is possible of existence.
XX The converse, what is necessary of existence has no
cause.   XXI Whatever is composite, the composition is
its cause of existence, and therefore possible, as evidenced
from above.   XXII Body is composed of matter and form
by necessity, and is the bearer of some accidents by
necessity.   XXIII. Whatever is possible, even if the
possibility is internal, and the thing does not need any
external force for realization, yet it is possible that it
should not exist.[21] XXIV. Whatever is potential is material

---

[14] *Ibid*   [15] *Physics*, VIII, 8.

[16] *Ibid*, VIII, 7   [17] *Ibid*, IV, 12

[18] כל מה שאינו גוף לא יושכל בו מנין, literally, in whatever is not
a body enumeration cannot be conceived, *Metaph*, XII, 8

[19] כי כל מה שיצא מן הבח אל הפועל מוציאו זולתו ונומר, *Moreh*,
II, 9, *Physics*, VII, 1

[20] *Metaph* XII, 2

[21] In the translation of this proposition I have followed Hasdai Crescas's

XXV. The elements of a composite body are matter and form, and therefore a body is in need of an agent to unite them. XXVI. Time and motion are eternal [22]

THE LOGICAL CONSEQUENCES OF THE PROPOSITIONS.

In basing his proofs of the existence of God and the theory of attributes, Maimonides does not start from the first proposition, but on the contrary from the twenty-fifth. This proposition, which is in turn based on the twenty-second which states that a body is composite by necessity, and on the fifth which defines the nature of motion as the process of realization, says. Every composite body in order to become needs a mover. Since all bodies in the perceptible world are composite, it is necessary to look for their causes or movers. This series of causes cannot go on to infinity, as has been demonstrated in the third proposition. Again, in regard to movements, we found in proposition IV that there are four kinds, and of these locomotion is the earliest, as shown in proposition XIV, and the circular the most perfect. The movement of the first sphere is then the cause of all movement in this world. However, by the same force of reasoning we are compelled to search for the mover of this sphere We have seen in proposition XVII that a body may be moved either by an external cause or an

ומה שיראה לנו בביאור זאת where he says, 12 b, אור ה', interpretation in
ההקדמה כפי מה שאומר. כל מה שהוא בכח דבר והאפשרות ההוא הוא
בעצמו וזה שהאפשרות הוא בכח דבר ממנו שהאפשרות בעצמו כאילו
תאמר שיהיה אפשר בעצמו שישתנה וישוב לבן ואפשר שיהיה האפשרות
נתלה בדבר חוץ ממנו כאלו תאמר שאפשר בשישחיר שישחיר בתנאי
שיהיה המקבל נשם לח.

[22] *Physics*, VIII, 1

W   D

internal one. The cause of movement of the first sphere
cannot be inherent in itself, since by proposition XXVI we
know that movement is eternal, and thus it is infinite;
the moving force of the first sphere then would have to be
infinite, but this is impossible. It was shown in proposition I
that no infinite body exists , the first sphere then is a finite
body. But as such it cannot have any infinite force, for
it was proved in proposition XII that no finite body can
have an infinite force inherent in it. It follows that the
cause of movement of the first sphere is an external one [23]
We have, then, established the proof of the existence of
a prime mover. It must be the prime, for otherwise we
shall have an infinite causal series.

The nature and character of the mover can also be
deduced from the same propositions. The external prime
mover cannot be corporeal, for then, according to the ninth
proposition, it would be moved while moving, and necessarily it would require another body as its mover, and thus
ad infinitum, but this is impossible (prop. III).   Again,
since it is incorporeal it is also unmoved, for movements
are either essential to bodies or accidental, and the prime
mover not being a body does not move either essentially
or accidentally. Further, since it is unmoved it is also indivisible and unchangeable, for, according to proposition VII,
whatever is not divisible does not move and is not a body,
the converse of it being equally true   From the force of
the same conclusions follows also the unity of the prime

[23] יתחיב בהכרח לפי זה הדעת שתהיה הסבה הראשונה לתנועת הגלגל
ר"ל נבדל מן הגלגל כמו שחייבתהו החלוקה   The word נבדל here means
not only external but incorporeal   But for the sake of clearness of thought
we prefer to treat of the incorporeality in the next paragraph. *Moreh*, II,
13 b , *Guide*, p. 16.

mover. There is only one, for in accordance with proposition XVI, whatever is neither a body nor a force inherent in a body does not fall under the category of number. We have then established the existence of God, His incorporeality, indivisibility, immutability, and unity.[24]

Maimonides quotes also several other proofs borrowed from Aristotle's works, one from the *Metaphysics*. It is the one mentioned above. There must be an unmoved mover, for since we find a moved mover, and we also find a thing moved and not moving, it follows that there must be an unmoved mover; as it is proved that when we find a thing composed of two elements, and then we find one element alone, it follows that the other element must also be found alone. The nature of the first cause is deduced from the fact that it is unmoved, in the same way as above.[25] In his third proof, Maimonides follows closely the Aristotelian found in *Metaphysics*, book XII, ch. vi. There must be one substance necessary of existence, otherwise the world of things would be destructible.[26] The third proposition is again utilized, for there cannot be an infinite regressus of possibles. Since it is necessary of existence through itself it is incorporeal, for according to proposition XXI, the composition of a body is the cause of its existence. The rest of the qualities follow necessarily. Maimonides quotes also a fourth proof which adds nothing new, but repeats the same argument in a different form. Maimonides

---

[24] *Moreh*, II, p. 13 b., *Guide*, II, p. 16

[25] *Moreh*, II, p. 14 a., *Guide*, II, pp. 17 sq

[26] א״כ יתחיב בהכרח בזה העיון אחר שיש נמצאות הוית נפסדות כמו שנראה שיהיה נמצא אחד לא הווה ולא נפסד, זה הנמצא שאינו לא הווה ולא נפסד אין אבשרות הפסד בו כלל אבל הוא מחויב המציאות לא אפשר המציאות, *Moreh*, II, 15 a

produces two more proofs for the oneness of God. Of
these two, one is mentioned by Saadia and Bahia. Suppose
there were two Gods, there would have to be at least one
point of difference between them and some points of
similarity in as far as both are Gods. This would involve
the existence of two elements in the nature of the Gods,
and thus they would be composite. The second proof is
from the harmony and uniformity of the sum total of
existence   This bears evidence to the oneness of God.
If there were two Gods, there ought to be either a division
of labour or collaboration, for the interdependence testifies
to one plan   But the first is impossible, for then God
would not be all-potent, and, consequently, there would be
a cause restraining the Divine power; but this is contrary
to the concept of God. This argument is also brought
by Saadia, but Maimonides gives it a more Aristotelian
form [27]

In comparing Maimonides' proofs with the proofs of
those who went before him, we see that, while he did not
contribute much originality to the problem, he at the same
time systematized and arranged the proofs in complete
logical order, which made them convincing. Most of the
antecedent philosophers either omitted some links in the
logical chain, such as the impossibility of an infinite causal
regressus, or hinted at it without making their thoughts
clear. Maimonides, as a careful builder, included everything.
In regard to Aristotle, he exhibits himself a faithful
follower, without accepting the conclusion at which he
arrives.

[27] *Moreh*, II, 16 a-b, *Guide*, p 23

PROOFS OF THE ARISTOTELIAN PROPOSITIONS.

Aristotle proves that the infinite does not exist either as a separate independent thing, or as a sensible thing, or as a movable   The infinite, says Aristotle, may be of several kinds, either such that it is not in its nature to be measured or passed through, as the voice is invisible,[28] or such one that cannot be passed through on account of its extent.[29] It is the last kind of infinite that the discussion turns on, for the first kind of infinite cannot be a principle nor an element.   There cannot be a separate independent infinite as a thing by itself, for it must be either divisible or indivisible.   If it is indivisible, it cannot be infinite except in the same way as the voice is indivisible, which is a quality that does not belong to it by nature , but we speak of an impassable infinite, which implies extent, and thus it is coupled with magnitude   But if it is divisible, it is a quantity and cannot exist by itself.   Again, if it is divisible and exists as a substance, every part of it will be infinite, and this is absurd, for there cannot be many infinities in one.   It must, therefore, be indivisible, but it is magnitude, and magnitude does not exist by itself.   It must, therefore, be an accident, but then it is not a principle, nor a separate.[30]

There cannot be an infinite body: first, it is impossible by the mere definition of a body which describes it to be a thing that has superficies bounded by planes, and this

---

[28] *Physics*, III, 5 ; *Metaph* , book K, ch. x.

[29] Spinoza, in his *Epistola XII, Opera*, ed. Van Vloten and Land, Hague, 1882, makes a similar distinction, calling the first infinite, the second indefinite.

[30] *Physics*, III, 5 ; *Metaph.*, book K, ch x.

already implies finitude. There are, however, more concrete arguments. An infinite body could be neither simple nor composite, for if the elements are finite, one at least must be infinite, and then the others will be destroyed since the infinite element must surely have most potency. If all the elements were infinite, the infinite body would be composed of many infinities, which is absurd. Simple it cannot be, for it is not of the four elements, since they are all finite and there are no other elements beside them. Again, how could anything be created, for becoming implies change from one contrary to another, and infinite has no contraries. It is evident, therefore, that there cannot be a simple infinite body.

Further, if there is an infinite body, it must have weight, whether light or heavy, but this is impossible, for the light moves upwards and the heavy downwards, but the infinite has neither an 'up' nor a 'down'. Again, since every body is in place, infinite body must have infinite place, but there is not any infinite place, since there are six kinds of place, the up and the down, &c. Finally, since body must be in place, and the latter by definition is the limit of the surrounding body, body must be finite.[31]

It is also impossible that there should exist a moving infinite, whether moving in rectilinear fashion or circular. Every body has a definite place, and the place of the part and the whole is the same. Consequently, an infinite body cannot move rectilinearly, as it is composed either of like parts or unlike parts. If of like parts, no part can move, for the place of the part is the place of the whole and it is infinite. If of unlike parts, the parts must be either finite or infinite; if finite, then at least one is infinite in magnitude,

<hr />

[31] *Physics*, III, 5; *Metaph*, book K, ch x.

and this is impossible.[32]   If they are infinite in number, then there are an infinite number of places, but this is impossible.[33]   Again, an infinite body must have infinite weight, and because of it its moving is unthinkable.   The heavier a body is the less the time in which it moves.   It follows that an infinite body must either move in no time or the 'now', which is the same, or that if we posit for it some time we will find a finite body moving in the same time   The relation of time and weight is a reverse one. Now if we posit some time for the infinite, it is possible to find a finite body of whatever weight moving in the same time.   We have then a finite and infinite body moving in the same ratio of time: this is contrary to the principles of motion.   Still more, if we multiply the body of finite weight, it will move in less time than the body of infinite weight, but such a supposition is absurd.

Likewise, the circular movement of an infinite body is impossible, for if the circle is infinite, the radii are also infinite and the distance infinite ; the circle then would never be completed and the distance never measured through. Again, the time of the revolution of a circle is finite, but the distance in this case is infinite , how then can infinite distance be traversed in finite time?[34]   Finally, it is impossible for the infinite to be either an active agent or a patient.   The relation between two bodies, one affecting and the other affected, is the following .   Two bodies equally large will both be affected in an equal time ; if one is smaller, it is affected in less time.   The relation also varies according to the power of the agent, and the

---

[32] Cp above, this section.

[33] *De Coelo*, ed. Prantl, I, ch 7 , *Physics,* III, 5 , *Metaph* , book K, ch x.

[34] *De Coelo,* I, ch 5

affection must be accomplished in a certain limited time. It follows, therefore, that the infinite can neither affect nor be affected, for since we must posit for it a certain time' as it cannot be affected nor affect in no time, we can always find a certain finite body that is either affected or affects in a similar amount of time. Moreover, if the finite body is increased in size, it will be affected or affect in a longer or a shorter time respectively than the infinite body. But this is contrary to the principle of action and passion.[35]

These, in short, are the arguments of Aristotle against the infinite, which are very accurately reproduced by Crescas He shows an extensive acquaintance with Aristotle's works hardly displayed before by any Jewish philosopher He now launches his criticism against each of the arguments, examining it in detail

CRESCAS'S REFUTATIONS OF ARISTOTELIAN ARGUMENTS

Crescas, in attacking Aristotle, follows the latter's arguments in logical order. First, Aristotle argues that there is no separate infinite as a thing in itself, for if it does exist and is divisible, its parts would have to be infinite (cp above). This, replies Crescas, does not necessarily follow. Since the infinite we are speaking of is a separable, not a corporeal one, why should it be divisible or its parts infinite? Is the mathematical line divisible, and are its parts points? Why can there not be an indivisible infinite?[36]   But the main force of the Aris-

[35] *Ibid.*, p. 273

[36] ונאמר שהמוכת ההוא הוא הטבעי ונערך על הדרוש וזה שחמניח גודל בלתי ב"ת אמר במציאות שעור נבדל ולזה נ"כ לא יתחיב שגדר

totelian argument against the existence of a separate
infinite, as Crescas rightly observes, consists in the impossibility of the existence of a separate magnitude not
connected with a body (cp above). A magnitude cannot
exist separately, for then space would have to exist
separately of the body, but according to the Aristotelian
conception of space it is impossible. Outside of the world
nothing exists, there is no vacuum stretching beyond its
boundaries, and, since whatever is in the world is body,
it follows that if we do conceive any magnitude, we must
conceive it in bodily form ; hence there is no separate
magnitude, and, consequently, no separate infinite

But, says Crescas, this line of reasoning is a *petitio
principii*, as the conclusion is still to be established , for
should we prove the existence of a vacuum there is a
possibility for an infinite to exist. Crescas then proceeds
to refute Aristotle's contention of the non-existence of the
infinite, attacking the basic principle There is no vacuum,
argues Aristotle, for if there were, movement in it would
be impossible. Movement in space is caused by the
difference in the natural inclination of things to strive
towards certain points some tending upwards, some downwards; the vacuum has no such places. A body in it
would either never move, for why should it move in one
direction rather than in the other, or never stop, since

הבב"ת יצדק על במו שלא יתחיב זה בקו הלמודי, *Or Adonai*, p 14 a.
Spinoza, in his *Epistola XII*, in discussing the infinite, produces the same
argument 'Quare omnis illa farrago argumentorum quibus substantiam
extensam finitam esse, philosophi vulgo moliuntur sua sponte ruit Omnia
illa substantia corpoream ex partibus conflatam supponunt ad eundem etiam
modum alii qui postquam sibi persuaserunt, lineam punctis componi multa
invenire potuerunt argumenta quibus ostenderunt lineam non esse in
infinitam divisibilem' *Opera*, II, p 42

there is no tendency to a certain place.[37]   Again, not only
could there not be natural motion, but not even violent
motion   Projectiles thrown by a person or instrument
continue their motion after the motor ceased to have
contact with them, because the particles of the air are
moved, and they impart the motion continually to the
projectile. But in a vacuum the motion cannot be con-
veyed ; the projectile must therefore stop of necessity.

Further, the rate of motion varies according to the
power of the motor and according to the media and their
power of resistance. The thinner the medium, the more
accelerated is the motion.   If a vacuum exists, motion
in it would have to take place in no time.   Two bodies,
A and B, move in different media, C and D. If the motors
are equal, the rate of time and motion of A and B will vary
according to C and D.   But if D is a vacuum, there is no
ratio, for what comparison could there be between the
motion of B which is not offered any resistance whatever,
and that of A which has to overcome it in a degree?
The movement of B, therefore, will be in no time.   But
movement must be in time , a vacuum, therefore, does not
exist.   Finally, if a vacuum exists, it is possible for two
bodies to occupy one place.   When anything is thrown
into water, an amount of water equal to the body is dis-
placed, and a similar process takes place in air   What then
will happen to a body in a vacuum ? If the vacuum merely
recedes then it is nothing ; it is just this that we endeavoured
to prove.   But if the vacuum is something, it must permeate the body ;[88] why then should not any body permeate

[37] *Physics*, IV, 7

[88] *Physics*, IV, 8   See also Simplicius's commentary to that chapter,
translated by Thomas Taylor in his translation of the *Physics* of Aristotle.
London, 1806, p 228

another body? The reason that body does not permeate body is not because of its substance or colour but because of its distance or intervals. Now if the intervals of the vacuum may permeate a body, why not any other intervals?

These arguments Crescas attempts to disprove in the following manner It does not follow, says he, that the existence of a vacuum should prevent motion. It is true that a vacuum does not possess any differences of a spatial nature such as upwards and downwards, but still, as long as the points of natural tendency exist and the elements possess that tendency, they will go on moving though the medium of movement is a vacuum. As for violent motion, it seems that the moment a body is set in motion, it acquires by virtue of its elements and their tendency towards their natural place a propensity to move without any assistance on the part of the medium. Further, argues Crescas, granted that rectilinear motion cannot be in a vacuum, still what is there to prevent the existence of an extra-mundane vacuum, wherein a body can move in a circular fashion, a movement which does not necessitate the possession of the *termini a quo* and *ad quem*.[39] In regard to the second argument of Aristotle, Crescas contends that it is based on a false premise The argument assumes that the ratio of the motion of one body to the motion of the other is as medium to medium, when

[39] ואם חיו מעורבין (כלומר היסודות) ברקות היית להם האותות במקומם הטבעי וחלוף טבע מה שממנו ומה שאליו לסבת קרובו או רחוקו מהמקיף או מהטרכז. ולזה לא מנע מציאות התנועה הטבעית וההכרחית במציאות הרקות וכ"ש שלא יחויב בזה המופת המנועות מציאות הרקות חוץ לעולם, למה שאם היה הרקות שאין לו טבע ממה שמנו ומה שאליו לא יתחיב המנועות תנועה סבובית לנשם כדורי   *Or Adonai,* p. 14b

media aie different in density, but this is untrue. We, asseits Crescas, must grant to every moving body an original motion which was imparted to it by the motor varying according to the strength of the motor. The medium only retards the motion by its resistance but it cannot accelerate it. The formula, therefoie, ought to be: the ratio of retaidation of one body to the retardation of another body varies as the media   In a vacuum, theiefore, resistance is reduced to zeio, but the original motion is preseived, and the body is still moved in a ceitain time. Finally, the aigument of the impenetiability of matter (cp above) is objected to by Crescas. Aristotle's dictum that body cannot penetrate body on account of its distances and dimensions cannot be tiue, for a body is impenetrable not on account of its possessing mere distances, but because of the matter filling those distances. Immateiial distances, such as the interval which is called a vacuum, may peimeate a body   It is evident, therefore, that a vacuum may exist. Fuither evidence of its existence is the fact that it is quantitatively conceived, as, for instance, if the air in a vessel is partly pumped out, we say that the vacuum is large oi small accoiding to the amount of air pumped out. It is then necessarily a magnitude, and though gianting that there is not an infinite body, the existence of a separable infinite magnitude is still more necessitated. Beyond the world there is no body, the vacuum cannot be limited by body, but it surely cannot be limited by a vacuum, it must be infinite.[40]

While these objections hardly have any value in the light of modern science, yet according to the spirit of the times they aie valid, and greatly testify to the critical

[40] *Or Adonai, ibid*, 15 a

ability and analytic acumen of Crescas.   They surely form
a step in the formation of the right scientific cosmogony.
The conceptions of the infinity of the world and of the
existence of infinite space were necessary conditions in
the generation of the Copernican system and the new
cosmological view   Surely, Crescas as well as Aristotle
was ignorant of the real laws of motion.   It is remarkable
that Aristotle, who had a notion of the law of inertia as
seen from his arguments against the existence of a vacuum,
namely, that if a vacuum exists perpetual motion were
possible, for in vacuo a body may move on for ever, and
who also recognized the resistance of air as evidenced from
his second argument against the existence of a vacuum,
should not have discovered the law of inertia and have
considered the particles of air as helping motion rather
than impeding it, yet in Crescas's refutation we perceive
a glimpse of the law of gravitation.   It is not known
whether Crescas ever exerted any influence upon Giordano
Bruno or not, though another Italian, Franz Pico, quotes
his anti-Aristotelian arguments in full,[41] but whatever be
the case, it is interesting to observe the similar pulsations
of mental activity in different ages, periods, and lands.

Crescas next proceeds to refute Aristotle's arguments
against the existence of an infinite body.   The latter's
general argument from the definition (cp. above) of body
as a thing that has limited superficies, says Crescas, is only
a *petitio principii*[42]   It is just this limitation that we seek
to establish   The one who asserts the existence of an
infinite body denies the assumed definition.   But, says he
further, his other arguments are also not proved.   The

[41] M. Joel in his *Chasdai Crescas*, note iv, Anhang.
[42] In Crescas's words it is termed מערכה על הדרוש.

infinite, says Aristotle, cannot be a composite, for if it is,
the elements would have to be infinite, and this is impossible.
Crescas rejoins, The impossibility of the existence of infinite
elements is not established, the reason, according to
Aristotle, for the non-existence is that the infinite cannot
be conceived, but, asks Crescas, must they be conceived
in order to exist?[43]   The elements *qua* elements may have
existence though not exactly known   This objection marks
a departure from the dominant Aristotelian system which
ascribed existence only to such things that were supported
by the evidence of the senses and logical reasoning.   Such
a conception could hardly be grasped by an Aristotelian.
That a thing in itself, to use the Kantian terminology, may
exist without being either perceived or logically analysed
or described, was an impossibility to them.[44]

Further, says Crescas, the objection that if the infinite
is composite, one element at least must be infinite and then
it would destroy the rest, can be answered in this way,
that the infinite may be devoid of qualities just as the
heavenly spheres are.   However, here Crescas seems not
to understand Aristotle.   Aristotle, in *Metaphysics*, book K,
ch. x, states distinctly that one element must not fall short
in potency, and whatever is in potency must sometimes be
realized, so that finally it will destroy the other element[45]
Crescas probably thought that it meant the infinite element
would have stronger actual qualities.   Again, Aristotle's
argument for the impossibility of the existence of an

---

[43] והנה אין מחברח ההתחלות במה שהן התחלות להאמן ידועות וזה
מבואר בעצמו, *Or Adonai*, p 15.

[44] *Or Adonai*, p 15 a.

[45] Cp Brandis, in his *Handbuch der Geschichte der Griechisch-Römischen
Philosophie*, II, p 727, *Physics*, IV, 5.

infinite body on account of its weight and its tending to
its natural places (cp. above) is not unimpeachable   Why,
asks Crescas, must it have weight?   Is it not because all
sensible bodies in the sublunar sphere have it?   But suppose
the infinite is different, is not the matter of the heavenly
spheres, according to Aristotle, devoid of weight?[46]   This
is another indictment against the following of the chain
of evidence of the senses and logical reasoning.

Finally, Crescas directs his main attack against the
arguments from the nature of space   Aristotle defines
space as the limit of the containing body,[47] and consequently by its very definition and nature it must be finite
and inherently connected with body   Where there is no
body there is no space, and, therefore, the world as a whole
is not in space though its parts are.   This theory, says
Crescas, is untenable.   The whole conceptual structure of
Aristotle of natural places, of upwards and downwards,
and the tendency of various elements thereto, is built on
false premises.   How, asks he, can we assert that air has
a natural place, the ' up ', near the fiery sphere?   What
happens then to the middle layers of air?   Are they in their
natural place? but it was asserted that their natural place
is the ' up '.   If they are not in their natural place, we have
then a phenomenon of variance of places, the place of the
part differing from the place of the whole.[48]   Again,

[46] ואולם האומר בנשם בב"ת ואמר שאין לו כובד ולא קלות כמו
שיאמר בגרמים השמימיים לדעת אריסטו, *Or Adonai*, p 15a

[47] *Physics*, IV, 3

[48] וזה שמקום האויר עד"ס לפי סברתי הוא השטח המקיף בקערירות
האש למה שיש לו שם ערבות ורמיון,   ואמנם החלק האמצעי מן האויר
לא נמלט אם שהוא במקומו הטבעי.   אם שאינו במקומו הטבעי יתחיב
שמקומו הטבעי אשר לחלק יתחלף למקום הטבעי אשר לכל והוא בתכלית
הגנות, *Or Adonai*, p 15f.

the place of the element of earth is the 'down'. But the absolute down is only a point,[49] and a point is not in place.[50] Crescas, therefore, proposes a different definition of place. It is, as we should say, a receptacle of things, qualityless, immovable, and indescribable. It is infinite, for by its very nature it cannot be finite.[51] In the world of things it is occupied, but beyond the world it exists as empty space. The fact that place is immovable answers Aristotle's arguments against defining place as an interval. Such a definition, says Aristotle, would compel us to admit the existence of a place to place, for if we move a vessel full of water, the interval of the vessel is transferred into another interval, and so on. But if we assume with Crescas that place is immovable, the difficulty disappears, for the vessel simply passes from one part of the universal vacuum to another. As for the water in the vessel, it is moved accidentally by the movement of the vessel. Aristotle explains the movement of the water in the same way.[52]

The refutation of Aristotle's assertion of the impossibility for an infinite body to move either in a rectilinear or circular fashion runs in the following manner. Aristotle's first argument that the infinite cannot move rectilinearly, for this movement requires an 'up' and a 'down', and is therefore a limited movement, can be obviated by replying that though kinds of places may be conceptually limited in genus, yet they are not so in species. In other words,

[49] *De Coelo*   [50] *Or Adonai*, p. 15 b

[51] שהמקום האמתי לגשם הוא הפנוי השוה לגשם אשר יטרידני הגשם, *Or Adonai*, p 14 b, again, שהמקום האמתי לדבר הוא חרחקי אשר בין שהמקום, *ibid*, p 15 b. Cp above Crescas's arguments about the vacuum

[52] Simplicius *ad locum* quoted by Thomas Taylor, *The Philosophy of Aristotle.*

there is no absolute point where we may say that this is the 'up', but there may be a series of 'ups' *ad infinitum*; the term 'up' being only our subjective designation.   His second argument (cp. above) that if there exists an infinite body it would have infinite weight, and then would move in the 'now' is irrelevant, says Crescas.   Since movement of a body must be in time, we shall have to posit a certain minimum for an infinite body.   It is true that a finite body may be found that will move in the same time.   But what of it?   The law of relations of movement to movement, according to the weight, extends only down to a certain point [53]   Of course, Crescas shows here a poor conception of law, but a more accurate conception could hardly be expected in his time.

Crescas also attempts to disprove the Aristotelian arguments against the possibility of an infinite body moving in a circular fashion   Aristotle says that there can be no circular movement, because the distance between two radii would be infinite, and it is impossible to traverse an infinite distance.   To this Crescas rejoins that, though the lines may be infinite, yet the distance between them may be finite.   The arguments, however, are too obscure and abstruse to reproduce here, and as they affect the subject very little we may omit them.   He seems to imply that there is a possibility of an infinite body moving in an incomplete circle, so that parts of it may move a finite distance.   But how he could at all conceive of the movement of an infinite body is difficult to see, for granted that there is an infinite space, the infinite body occupies it all by virtue of its own definition   And what meaning has movement, unless we assume the modern conception of

[53] *Or Adonai*, p. 16 a.

a growing infinite, but this is hardly what Crescas means. However, Crescas wrote many things for the sake of argument, simply to show that what Aristotle said can be refuted, just as Aristotle himself multiplied unnecessary arguments. What is important for us is the establishment of the theory of infinite space, and the possibility of an infinitude of magnitudes. This leads, as Crescas well saw,[54] to the possibility of the existence of other worlds besides this one, a conjecture which was later well established. Especially important is his remark against Aristotle's arguments, that if there were many worlds the elements would move from one to the other Why should they? asks Crescas Is it not possible that the elements we know exist only in this world, and the other worlds have different elements and different tendencies? We notice here the beginning of the fall of the Aristotelian cosmology, based on the evidence of senses only, an event which was delayed for some time but accomplished in full by such masters as Copernicus, Giordano Bruno, and Galileo.

The second proposition, that it is impossible for an infinite number of finite magnitudes to exist, stands and falls with the first The criticism of the third proposition, the impossibility of an infinite causal regressus, is interesting. Crescas does not refute it entirely, it being necessary for his proof of the existence of God, as will be shown. He does give it a different interpretation. Why, asks Crescas, can there not be an infinite number of effects which are at the same time causes to each other? It is true that we must posit one prior cause, but that should not prevent

[54] וזה שכבר התבאר במה שקדם חיוב מציאות נודל בלתי בעל תכלית וחיוב ריקו או עלוי בלתי בעל תכלית חוץ לעולם הוא מבואר שמציאות עולמים רבים אפשר, *Or Adonai*, p 17 a

the posterior causes from being infinite. Aristotle's argument that every intermediate term must be preceded by a first,[55] would be well applicable if the causal series were a timely one, namely, that each event in the series must precede the other in time. But the relation of cause and effect is really one of logical priority. Aristotle himself argues for the eternity of the world, and is therefore forced to admit that the first cause is only prior in a logical sense and not in time, as the first sphere is also eternal Why can we not say that out of the first cause there emanated an infinite number of effects which exist simultaneously, instead of one effect as Aristotle wants us to believe? And since an infinite number of effects is possible, what prevents us from assuming that the effects are also causes to one another, since causal priority does not posit temporal precedence?[56] Of course, in spite of Crescas's criticism, the necessity of a first cause, first in necessity, is well established, but the form is changed, and has an important bearing upon the whole conception of infinity The manner in which Crescas utilized this proposition for the proof of the existence of God, so very different from the customary peripatetic way, was commended by Spinoza.[57] Aristotle was not entirely ignorant of the weakness of his assertion, and in *Metaphysics*, book XII, ch. vi, he mentions a similar interpretation to that of Crescas, but in his main discussions in *Metaphysics* his language shows the contrary.

The eighth proposition stating that whatever moves accidentally will eventually rest of necessity, which forms

[55] *Metaphysics*, I a or II

[56] והנה בשנניח ג"כ העלולים הבב"ת כל אחת עלה לחברו לא יקרה מזה שום בטול אלא שאנו צריכים לדבר יכריח מציאותם על העדרם אחר שכלם אפשרי המציאות, p. 17 b.

[57] *Opera*, V, 11 ; *Epistola XII*

a link in the proof of the existence of God, is severely scrutinized by Crescas. Is it not possible, asks he, that accidents exist as long as the substance itself; now if the substance is eternally moved, why not the accidents? Do not the lower spheres move eternally, because of the essential movement of the first sphere, though their own movement is accidental? The crucial point of the Aristotelian argument is, that since a mover while moving another body is moved itself, a power in a body while it moves the body is also moved accidentally, and consequently it will have to rest of necessity. Crescas says, It does not follow necessarily, for as long as the body can be moved eternally, why should the movement of the force ever have to stop since it is connected with the essential movement of the body?[58]

His criticism of the tenth proposition is interesting though of little importance for the subject. It relates to the famous Aristotelian theory that form is the stay of body. Crescas, after quoting Ibn Roshd, who asserts that body by evidence of sense is really one but logic forces us to admit composition because of its corruptibility, asks, Why can we not conceive matter as having a certain form by itself, the corporeality, for instance, consisting in a kind of general quality such as occupying space? Of course, when we contemplate a particular piece of matter we find it to have a particular form, but this is only the individual form, and while essential yet is not the stay of the body, for the material form is always in existence and is really the bearer of the individual form.[59] This remark, though short, is very suggestive. It reminds us of the Cartesian principle that all matter is extension.

[58] *Or Adonai*, 18 a   [59] *Ibid*, 18 b

Crescas, in his refutations, attacks also the twelfth proposition, which is of great importance in the Maimonidian proof of the existence of God. The proposition asserts that every force in a finite body is finite. It is based on the assumed relation of motion to force The rate and time of a moved body varies inversely to the force moving it. The greater the force, the less the time. If there exists an infinite force in a finite body, that body will either be moved in the ' now ' or a finite force will be equal in moving power to an infinite. (Cp. above, Aristotle's proof of the impossibility of an actual infinite.) Crescas first refers to his refutation of the above-mentioned argument in regard to the infinite moving in ' now ', where he contends that since movement must be in time there is a minimum which is necessary even for an infinite. The law of the relation of time to force will be valid only above that minimum.[60]   In addition, says Crescas, granted that the relation holds true as regards the strength or celerity of the motion, still since there can be an infinite movement in time, why cannot the force of a finite body, having a definite and limited rate of motion, move a body infinitely, when there is no cause for its ceasing, and no resistance impeding it ?   Especially such bodies as the heavenly spheres which are of an ethereal substance, and consequently offer no resistance, could be moved eternally even by a finite force. This critical remark displays a quite advanced conception of motion and resistance, more penetrating than that of Aristotle, who related the continuity of motion to the force and employed the assumed relation as a cardinal proof of the existence of a first mover.

[60] למה שיחס הכח אל הכח יהי בומן העודף על זמן השרשי הידוע
אצל הטבע, *Or Adonai*, p 18 b

Finally, the Aristotelian conception of time is attacked
(This forms proposition XV.) Time, says the Stagyrite,
is an accident of motion, and cannot be conceived without
it. This statement comprises four premisses. 1. Time is
an accident joined to movement; 2. either is not found
without the other; 3. and is not conceived without the
other, 4. and, finally, whatever has no movement is not
in time. But, rejoins Crescas, is not time a measure of
rest as well? Do we not measure the state of rest of a
body in time, whether it is long or short? The first two
premisses then fall The third, however, may be justified
if we define rest as the privation of motion. The conception
of time is joined to motion and not conceived without it,
though not always found together with motion. Crescas,
therefore, proposes a new definition of time. Time is the
concept of continuity of a certain state of a body, whether
it is movement or rest. It is true that time is an
accident, but an accident relating to the soul and
not to anything else [61] This conception of time is
quite a modern one, and reminds one of the Kantian
concept.

THE PROOFS OF MAIMONIDES REFUTED.

After attacking the individual links which make up
the Maimonidian proofs of the existence of God, Crescas
proceeds to demonstrate the results of the refutations
bearing on the proofs The first proof of Maimonides
(cp. above) makes essential use of the first proposition in

[61] ולזה הנדר הנכון בזמן יראה שהוא שעור התדבקות התנועה או
המנוחה שבין שתי עתות, *Or Adonai*, 19 a

connexion with the twelfth, for if there exists an infinite body it has infinite force, and so it can be self-moved, and there is no need of a first mover   Again, propositions II and III are necessary, for if there is an infinite causal regressus there is no first cause.   In the same way, several more propositions are needed   Since these propositions were refuted by Crescas (though proposition III, which is really the basic one, was not refuted, but given an entirely different interpretation), it follows that the proof as a whole is refuted   But, adds Crescas, even granting the truth of all these propositions, yet Maimonides has not established his case.   The twelfth proposition stating that a finite body must have a finite force, which is a cardinal point in the proof, does not establish the impossibility of a force in a finite body moving in an infinite time where there is no resistance ; though we may grant that the strength of the force is finite (cp. above). This objection alone is sufficient to overthrow the whole structure of the proof.   There is no necessity for a first unmoved mover, for the sphere can be moved by its own force infinitely.

Again, Maimonides has not established the unity of God.   He proves it by the sixteenth proposition, which asserts that whatever is neither a body nor a force in a body cannot be conceived under number unless it is a cause, and since there can be only one cause of that character to this world, the oneness of this cause follows.   But, says Crescas, this argument would be sufficient if we assume that there is only one world.   But since it was demonstrated (cp. above) that the existence of several worlds is possible, it is also possible that there should be several Gods. each one being a different cause of a different world in a different relation, and as such the Gods may be counted. Thus, the numerical unity is not proved [62]

The second proof of Maimonides is based on Aristotle's assertion that if we find a thing composed of two elements, and then one element alone, it follows that the other element must also exist by itself (cp above for the conclusion) The conclusion is attacked by Crescas, who says that logically it follows only that the separate existence of the other element is possible, but not that it is absolutely necessary He supports his contention by an illustration drawn from physiology as it was understood in his time. We know that all living beings are also vegetative as far as growth is concerned. We find, though, vegetation without life, but we never find living beings not having the vegetative quality (It is absurd, of course, from the modern point of view, that vegetation is a living organism.) We see, therefore, that it is not absolutely necessary for the two elements that compose a thing to exist separately, especially if one may act as a perfecting agent. The force of the Maimonidian argument is then broken [63]

The third argument of Maimonides, based on the assertion that all being cannot be perishable, since time and movement are eternal, is answered by Crescas in the following manner The imperishability of all being does not follow from the eternity of time and movement, for if we supposed that they would all perish at once, the argument would be valid, but why can there not be a continual series of perishable beings, one following another? The premiss, therefore, has not been established.[64] He advances also another argument against the proof, but it

---

[62] *Or Adonai,* 20 a. This subject will be discussed again in this chapter and in chapter II

[63] *Ibid ,* 20 b.   [64] *Ibid*

really has little force. In general, his refutation of the third proof is more for the sake of argumentation and logical casuistry than for the sake of serious discussion.   Crescas himself, as will be evidenced in the second chapter, proves the existence of God through a similar chain of argumentation, though with a different interpretation.   Finally, the last arguments of Maimonides are assailed.   The arguments centre about unity.   Crescas has already shown that Maimonides did not succeed in proving the oneness of the first cause.   He now elaborates the subject, and analyses the other arguments of Maimonides.   These arguments have often been quoted in Jewish as well as in scholastic philosophy, and run as follows (cp Introduction). The existence of two Gods is impossible for several reasons 1 If there were two, there would be a difference between them as well as a similarity; they would, therefore, be composite   2. The harmony of the world and the interdependence of beings testify to the existence of one God. 3. If there were two Gods, we should have to conclude that either one God created a part of the world and the other another, or that one worked for a certain time and the other for another period or that they co-operated.   All these results are absurd   It would follow that God is a composite, is in time and possible, which consequences are untenable (cp. Introduction, as well as above in the exposition of the Maimonidian theory for elucidation). But, rejoins Crescas, the conclusion, namely, the oneness of God, is not warranted.   First, the Gods must not be composite, for the difference between them need not be material; it may be only a causal one [65]   Second, since

ואם הב' כשנניח ההקדמות אמתיות הנה לא התבאר היותו א' וזה [65] שכבר יתחלפו בהיות א' עלה לאחר, *Or Adonai*, p 20 b

we may posit several worlds, we may also posit several Gods, each one having his world [66] This answers also the other arguments , for besides that the interdependence of this world of things does not prove anything, as there may be a pre-established harmony of plan between the Gods, it vanishes entirely with the assumption of the existence of several worlds, as it is evident. There are also other arguments quoted by Saadia and Bahia that are not affected by this assumption, but these arguments will be discussed in the second chapter together with the Spinozistic view on the subject.

We have reached a boundary line in Crescas's philosophy, namely, the end of his critical exposition of the proofs of the existence of God The point of view of Crescas has been mentioned before. It will suffice to remark in passing that his endeavour is to show the invalidity of many philosophic arguments concerning theological dogmas, so that necessarily we have to rely upon tradition. However, what has happened to many others has happened to him, that while their aim has not been reached, the very negative side is valuable. He displayed in his criticisms a keen sense of philosophic acumen and originality, and were this book more widely known, its influence on general thought would undoubtedly be greater. His anticipations of modern conceptions have already been noticed. Yet Crescas has value, not only in his negative criticisms but also in his positive conceptions. It will be evident in the future chapters. We thus pass on to the second chapter

[66] *Ibid.*, p 21 a

CHAPTER II

CRESCAS'S TREATMENT OF THE PROBLEMS RELATING TO THE EXISTENCE OF GOD AND HIS ATTRIBUTES.

THE existence of God is proved by Crescas in a veiy simple manner. The proof runs in the following way Whether there is a finite or an infinite numbei of effects, or whether an infinite series of causes is given, but as long as the series is infinite and all things are caused, we do not find in natuie a thing that is absolutely necessary of existence. But to conclude thus is impossible, foi if all beings are possible there must be some power that calls forth existence, so as to overbalance piivation It follows that there is a being necessary of existence [67] In this proof the force of the argument, as Spinoza well remarks, is not in the impossibility of an infinite act or an infinite causal regressus, but the stiess is laid on the absurdity of positing a world of possibles.[68]

[67] והנה אם שיהיו עלות ועלולים ב"ת או בב"ת אין המלט מהיות עלה אחת לכללם למה שאם היו כלם עלולים היו אפשרי המציאות בבחינת עצמם והם צריכים למכריע יכריע מציאותם על העדרם והעלה לכלם המכרעת מציאותם והוא האל י"ת, Or Adonai, Tr I, sect 3, ch. 2, p 22 a

[68] It will be best to quote Spinoza's own words on the subject 'Verum hic obiter adhuc notari velim quod peripatetici recentiores ut quidem puto, male intellexerint demonstrationem veterum qua ostendere nitebantur dei existentiam. Nam ut ipsam apud Iudaeum quendam Rab Ghasdai vocatim reperio, sic sonat, si dantur progressus causarum in infinitum, erunt omnia quae sunt, etiam causata Atque nulli quod causatum est competit, vi suae

Here may be considered the proper place to say a few words about the relation of Crescas to Spinoza. That the latter knew writings of the former and studied them, we know from the passage quoted, where Spinoza mentions Crescas by name, and very accurately explains the latter's proof of the existence of God. The question is whether Crescas really exerted any marked influence upon the formation of Spinoza's system   Joel endeavoured in several of his writings to establish that Spinoza was under the influence of Crescas, and attempted to trace the influence in some of Spinoza's important theories. It will be necessary for us to discuss these points of similarity as they come along   Kuno Fischer (in his *Geschichte der neueren Philosophie*, V, II, Spinoza) attempts to refute all arguments put forth in favour of influence, and concludes that there is nothing in common between them [60]

Fischer's arguments, however, do not seem conclusive. I wish to call attention to the first point in Spinoza's system namely, the existence of substance or God   The way Spinoza, in his *Ethics*, conceives the existence of ' a first cause is strikingly similar to that of Crescas. It is true that in the *Tractatus Brevis*, his first philosophical essay, Spinoza proves that God must exist, in the famous Cartesian way through the conception of the idea of God. But in the *Ethics* the basic conception of the whole system is that, in looking upon nature, we must come to the conclusion

naturae necessarie existere, ergo nihil est in natura ad cuius essentiam pertinet necessario existere   Sed hoc est absurdum , ergo et illud   Quare vis argumenti non in ea sita est, quod impossibile sit dari actu infinitum aut progressus causarum in infinitum , sed tantum in ea quod supponatur res quae sua natura non necessario existunt non determinari ad existendum a re sua natura necessario existent '   *Epistola XII*, ed Van Vloten, II, 45

[69] *Geschichte der neueren Philosophie*, II, pp 265-73.

that there must be a cause which is necessary of existence by itself 'This conception', says Kuno Fischer, 'which is put at the beginning of his philosophy, supports the whole system.'[70] Taking his first definition, 'By that which is self-caused, I mean that of which the essence involves existence', and his axiom, 'That which exists, exists either in itself or in something else'· again, axiom three, 'If no definite cause be granted, it is impossible that an effect can follow', as well as his proofs of proposition XI, we see clearly the underlying thought that in the world of things where there is a multitude of effects there must be something which is a *causa sui*. Placing the words of Crescas, 'Whether there be causes and effects finite or infinite, there is one thing clear, that there must be one cause for all, for if all are effects there would not be anything which is its own cause of existence,' besides this conception, one cannot help feeling the similarity between the initial points of these two philosophers, and the influence of the earlier upon the latter is not improbable The fact that Crescas and Spinoza are two opposite poles, the one religious to the extreme, the other irreligious, should not deter us. In spite of the fact mentioned, God is the very centre of things to both, and though, according to the latter, God acts in a mathematical way with absolute mechanical necessity, and, according to the former, in a personal way, yet the basic quality of God in both systems is the same, namely, absolute limitlessness, consequently, the philosophers concur in a goodly number of questions.

For this divergence in regard to religion really has nothing to do with the first conception of the existence of God. The conception itself is independent of religion,

[70] *Ibid*, p 358.

and might as well be taken by Spinoza as the basis of his system Fischer, as if feeling that in quoting Spinoza's letter where Crescas's proof is cited in such a way as to resemble Spinoza's own, he weakens his case, attempts to strengthen his arguments by alluding to the manner in which Spinoza speaks of Crescas. He names him 'quendam Rab Ghasdai'. Fischer infers that this proves sufficiently that Spinoza hardly knew Crescas and his teachings, and winds up by saying, 'Descartes was not a "quendam" to Spinoza.'[71] Such an argument is hardly conclusive. Spinoza wrote to Lewis Meyer, who surely hardly knew of Crescas, and to whom he was a 'certain'. But if Fischer were acquainted with the difficulty of Crescas's style and its remarkable brevity he would know that Spinoza could hardly give such a lucid and penetrating summary of Crescas's proof by mere hearsay without having studied his works carefully. Again, his additional remark (in *Ep. XII*, quoted above), 'non in ea sita est quod impossibile sit dari actu infinitum', shows that he read Crescas's whole refutation of the Aristotelian doctrine. The fact that Spinoza calls him a peripatetic, while Crescas combated the Aristotelian doctrines, is not sufficient evidence of his ignorance of Crescas's work. There was still left in Crescas enough of the philosophy of his time to entitle him to that name

ESSENCE AND EXISTENCE

It was an old debatable question with the mediaeval philosophers, whether existence is identical with the essence of a thing or is something separate Ibn Sina taught that

---

[71] *Geschichte der neueren Philosophie*, II, p 273

existence is an accident of essence.[72] Ibn Roshd, on the other hand, claimed that existence can be nothing else but identical with essence. According to Ibn Roshd and his followers then, in regard to God, since His essence is absolutely different from the essence of the rest of beings, it follows that His existence will also be different in kind, and in positing existence to both God and other beings we do so in an absolutely homonymous way, not denoting any common relation but the name.[73] But also the followers of Ibn Sina agree to this conception, for they concede necessarily that with God existence is not an accident, but identical with essence. And since with other beings it is only accidental, it follows that the name existence in applying it to God and to man is employed in an absolute homonymous way

Crescas does not agree with either view. In criticizing Ibn Roshd's view, he points out the logical difficulty involved in its assumption. If existence is identical with essence, what then does it add as a predicate? In stating that God exists, the predicate does not add anything, it amounts to saying, God is God. the same is true of any other proposition of the same kind. Again, if, as Ibn Sina says, existence is only an accident, it needs then a subject; but the subject must also exist, hence another subject must precede it, and so on to infinity. Again, since existence is the real form and stay of the subject, for without it it would be not-being, how could we call it accident? This view must necessarily be abandoned But the other view is untenable also. It must, therefore, be concluded that

---

[72] מו"נ פרק נ"ז ועיין פירוש קרשקש, *Moreh*, LVII (see also Crescas's Commentary), *Guide*, p 204.

[73] *Or Adonai*, p 21 b.

existence, while not identical with essence, is essential to a being.[74] In this way, existence can be predicated of everything, of the essence as well as of accidents, though there will be a difference of degree The general conception, however, must be understood in a negative way. The thing we predicate existence of is to be understood not non-existing. As a result, when we speak of the existence of God, and the existence of other beings, it must not be absolutely homonymous, but there may be a certain relation, namely, that the negation—for existing equals not non-existing—has a difference of degree. The not non-existence of God is due to himself, while of the other beings to their cause.[75] What Crescas wants to prove by his naming existence essential is that it is one of the expressions of essence, implying that there are more.

Spinoza seems to believe that existence and essence are different in the case of other beings, for essence depends on natural law, but existence on the order of the causal series. In God, however, existence is not distinguished from essence, for by definition, existence belongs to his nature.[76]

ATTRIBUTES AND UNITY

Maimonides' theory of Attributes, which is criticized by Crescas, resembles in its entirety the other theories of the preceding Jewish philosophers, with a strong emphasis on the negativity of their conception. A thing can be described, says he, in four ways, either according to its definition or

[74] וכאשר יתחיב שאיננו עצם המהות כמו שהתבאר מהספק הקודם הראשון ישאר א"כ שיחיה עצמי למהות, *Or Adonai*, p. 22 a

[75] *Ibid.*   [76] *Cogitata Metaphysica*, Part I, chs. 2, 3.

a part thereof, or by one of its essential qualities, or by relation to some other things, either to time, place, or another body.[77] In regard to God, attributes describing in any of the above-mentioned ways are inapplicable, for since we posit Him simple, and one, and above all categories, it is evident that He cannot be defined, nor can we speak of a part of Him nor of any essential quality in Him. As for relation, there is no relation between Him and place or time, or any other being, for they are all possible of existence and He is necessary. There remains, therefore, a fifth way of describing, namely, according to the actions   Such kind of attributes it is not impossible to apply to God, for they do not imply any plurality, change, or division. This form of attributes is paronymic, after the actions we perceive. There are, however, essential attributes, that is, such as appertain to the essence without having any bearing on the actions. Such by the consensus of religious leaders and philosophers are existent, living, knowing, wise, potent, and willing   It is to be noticed that Maimonides includes will as an attribute just as his peripatetic predecessor Ibn Daud has done, while Saadia and Bahia do not count it (cp. Introduction). How then shall we understand these essential attributes? Of course, it is evident that in applying them to both God and man we employ them in an absolute homonymic manner, for there is no possible relation between God and other beings   These attributes have to be conceived purely negatively, and yet, says Maimonides, they convey to us some positive notion. He proceeds to explain his assertion. The statement that God is existent implies only that He is not non-existing, or the denial of privation;

---

[77] מו"נ חלק א' פרק נ"ב, *Moreh*, I, 52 (p. 72 a), *Guide*, p 178

and when we say that God is living, we only assert that
His existence is not like the existence of dead matter.
In a similar way, the more difficult attributes are explained;
potent means the denial of weakness; wise, the privation
of foolishness, willing, the absence of disorder. This, in
short, is the Maimonidian theory of attributes.[78]

Gersonides, the immediate predecessor of Crescas, had
already objected to such a theory. He argued against the
assumption of absolute homonymity in applying the attributes to both God and man. It is impossible, he says,
to assume that there is only a likeness of name in the two
applications of the attribute, if it is construed to have a
negative meaning   Take, for example, the negative concept
of existing, can we say that the denial of non-existence
which the concept implies has two absolutely different
meanings? We are forced, then, to admit that the difference
is only in degree, why then can we not hold the same
conception in regard to positive attributes, namely, that
they are applied to God and to man in different degrees
of perfection?[79]   We have noticed a similar argument
advanced by Crescas in regard to existence. We shall
now pass on to Crescas's criticism of Maimonides' theory.
Maimonides is loath, says Crescas, to ascribe to God any
attributes that will bring Him in relation with something
else, for fear that it may imply a privation in His nature,

[78] ואמרנו בו מפני אלי העניגים שהוא יכול וחכם ורוצה, וחכונה באלו
התארים שאינו לואה ולא סכל ולא נבהל או עוב וענין אמרנו לא לואה
שמציאותו יש בה די להמצאת דברים אחרים זולתו, וענין אמרנו ולא
סכל שהוא משיג כלומר חי . . . , וענין אמרנו לא נבהל ולא עוב כי
כל אלה הנמצאות הולכות על סדר והנהנה, *Moreh*, p 86 b, *Guide*, P L.,
p. 210.

[79] *The Battles of the Lord*, II, p 134 (Milhamot, ed. Leipzig, 1866)

and yet he allows himself to describe Him with active attributes. But, asks Crescas, does the application of such attributes not imply any defect in God's perfection? When we say, God created or made, does it not mean that before the act His power was potential and only later became active? Such an implication suggests change in God's nature [80] Again, Maimonides' assertion that there is absolutely no relation between God and created beings or time is false. Is not God the cause of all existing being? But if He is, there is already a relation established, or if we assume that time is eternal, there is a relation of likeness between God and time. But Crescas sees as well as Maimonides the danger involved in ascribing to God positive attributes and at the same time asserting that He is simple and one. Yet, he says, there is really no contra-diction The fact that we humans may conceive plurality through attributes does not mean real plurality. His infinite goodness which is His essence unites them. Good-ness here should be understood to mean perfection, or in other words, God is infinitely perfect—what Spinoza calls in his writings the absolute perfect,[81] not perfect after its kind. Again, since God is indivisible and simple, and perfection is essential, then why cannot existence or any of the other attributes, as potence or wisdom, be posited as a positive attribute in just the same relation as light

[80] והנה אי אפשר לי מבלתי שנעיר דל ספקות שבאו בדבריו . . אם
תחלה אחר שהתארים שיתואר ביחסו לזולתו שביא להעדר נמנע מחקו
כמו שלא יהיה דבר בפעל לו ואח"ב ישוב בפעל הנה אך התיר מן החואר
שיתואר הדבר בפעולתו כאלו תאמר פעל ועשה ובּרא שזה כבר יביא אל
העדר שקודם הפעולה או העשיה או הבריאה כבר היה בכח ואח"כ שב
בפעל׳, Or Adonai, p. 23 a.

[81] Epistola XXXI, Opera, V, 11.

is posited of a luminous body? Let us, following up the analogy, suppose that the first cause is a luminous body, it is consequently necessary of existence. Is its light, though not identical with the essence of the body, less necessary of existence, or can the body not be described by it? The light is not a separate thing, but is an essential quality through which the body may be described. In a similar manner, we can call the attributes of God positive, especially such as eternity, existence, and unity, and yet they do not imply plurality.[82] It is true that so far as our conception is concerned we cannot give them a positive content, for that would determine God, and we must use the negative, e. g as existent, not non-existent, &c , but in regard to God himself they are surely positive, and He can be described by them [83]

Especially precarious is Maimonides' position, says Crescas, when we consider the other attributes such as wisdom and potence. What does he mean by saying that potence means absence of weakness, or knowing, privation of ignorance? He does not remove the positive content from the attribute. There is no *tertium quid* between knowing and not knowing, if not not-knowing; hence it necessarily follows that God is knowing. But if the attribute of knowing has a positive content, what then is that content? It is not identical with essence, for the essence of God is inconceivable in its totality; and surely it cannot

[82] לו הונח על דרך משל מאיר מהמחויב המציאות לעצמו המנע ממנו האור המתחיב ממנו בעצם חיוב המציאות אשר לו, לא כי האור איננו עצם נבדל מעצמותו שיהא צריך למרביב ומקבץ אבל הוא דבר עצמתי שראוי שיתואר בו בן הוא עניני התארים באל ית', *Or Adonai*, p. 24 b.
[83] *Ibid*

be an accident, for that is excluded from the conception.
It follows, therefore, that positive attributes are essential.
Again, he says, if we assume the Maimonidian view, it
follows that God will be absolutely qualityless, almost
equal to nothing, for, he says, if we deny any essential
attributes, it is not that we deny our knowledge of them,
but the having itself God will be then entirely negative,
neither potent nor impotent, nor anything, and this is
absurd. It is evident, therefore, that positive attributes
must be posited of God though we cannot determine
their content, and for human purposes may be described
negatively.[84]

As for unity, Crescas thinks that in a similar manner
to existence it is not essence, but essential. If we shall
say that it is essence, we shall encounter the same difficulty
in predication as in existence. When we say that man is
one, we do not state anything new about man, but merely
repeat that man is man. It follows, therefore, as has been
mentioned, that unity is an essential attribute and a
rational mode of conception. It follows also, since unity
is really a mode of differentiation, that God who is the most
differentiated of all other beings, is one par excellence.[85]

Crescas makes here a keen observation, namely, that
unity has a double meaning. It means simplicity, that the
object is not composite; and it is also to be understood
in a numerical sense, that there is only one God. Spinoza

[84] *Or Adonai*, p. 25 a–b

[85] ולוה הוא מבואר שאין היחור מקרה ולא דבר נוסף על העצם אלא
דבר עצמי אבל הנמצא בפעל ומוגבל ובחינת שבלית מהעדר הרבוי בו,
ובן להיות האהדות נותנת הנבלה והבדל לנמצא הוא מבואר שהנמצא
שהוא בתכלית התבדל מבל הנמצאות ואם היה שלא יפול בו הנבלה הנה
הוא יותר אמתי בשם האחד מזולתו, *Or Adonai*, p. 22 b.

expresses the latter by *unicum*.[86] As for the first, it was well established, for God is necessary of existence, and everything necessary of existence cannot be composite, as has been discussed.[87] The question remains in regard to the second. Is there only one God? We have shown above that Crescas always considered the arguments substantiating the oneness as insufficient. The interdependence of the world and the harmony of action are counterbalanced by his supposition of the possible existence of two worlds (cp. above). There is, however, one more argument, which says that since we posit the infinite potence of God, the existence of another God is impossible, for they would constrain each other. Yet, says Crescas, these arguments are not convincing, for it is still possible that the other one is not active. He, therefore, concludes that the numerical unity of God is only a subject of revelation.[88]

It must be admitted that Crescas in this point is not only weak, but prejudiced. His polemical nature overmastered the philosophical. What does he mean by a passive God? Does it not contradict his own conception of God? If God possesses infinite potence, what then is that other being? It is neither active nor potential. It is evident that this absurd argument was only advanced just as a shot at the philosophers, though it fell short of the mark, and Crescas well conceived it.

It is necessary, in conclusion of this part of Crescas's theory, to say a few words concerning his influence on Spinoza, regarding which there is some difference of opinion. Dr. Joel, in his book *Zur Genesis der Lehre Spinozas*,[89]

[86] *Cogitata Metaph.*, II, 2

[87] The same proof has been quoted by Spinoza

[88] *Or Adonai*, p 26 a.

[89] Pp. 19-24.

asserts that Spinoza was greatly influenced by Crescas in the formation of his theory of attributes. He says that Crescas makes a distinction between attributes of an essential nature and such as are rational modes of conception. Again, that this is the same distinction that Spinoza makes between attributes and propria,[90] namely, such qualities which are a part of God's own essence, though they do not affect His simplicity or immutability. It is difficult to agree with Joel, both that such a distinction is made by Crescas and that it is identical with Spinoza's Crescas calls both kinds of attributes, such as eternity, existence, and unity (rather simplicity), those that Joel would include in the second class, and knowledge or potency, which are, according to Joel, in the first class, by one name, namely, תוארים עצמיים,[91] which means essential attributes. It is true that Crescas says that the first-named attributes are less apt to affect the simplicity of God, for their content is only a rational mode with a negative form, as existence, not non-being, &c.[92] But no real distinction is found. He says distinctly, 'It is clear from the foregoing that existent and unity (simplicity), which are predicated of Him, His name be praised, are essential attributes',[93] or as Dr. Joel would express himself, 'wesenhafter Art'. Where then does Joel get his distinction? Again, Spinoza bases his distinction on the definition that the attributes, according to him, are identical with the essence of God which is

---

[90] *Or Adonai*, p. 25 a.

[91] *Korte Verhandeling*, Opera, p 274.

[92] וב"ש הקדמות שאיננו אלא בחינה שכלית שהוא בלתי הווה והמציאות שהוא הוראת היותו בלתי נעדר והאחדות שהוא מורה על היותו בזולת רבוי בעצמו ושהוא אין בו שניות בצד מן הצדדין, *Or Adonai*, p 24 b.

[93] *Ibid*, p. 25 a.

conceived through them, of such we know only two, thought and extension The Propria are such as belong to God, but do not express His essence.[94] Of such a distinction there is no mention in Crescas. On the contrary, Crescas asserts that the essence of God is inconceivable. This is really a fundamental difference between Crescas and Spinoza. Again, we find many of those Propria of Spinoza among the essential attributes, as, for instance, knowledge.[95] How, then, can we say that it is the same distinction? We can nevertheless admit that the idea found in Crescas that there are some attributes which, though predicated of God, do not by all means express His essence, is also found in Spinoza. But to consider it as a source of influence is exaggerating.

I want to direct attention to another point of contact between Crescas and Spinoza, which brings the possible influence into a more favourable light. It is the relation of the attributes to the essence of God. Crescas teaches the infinite perfection of God, and the absolute unity of His essence, in spite of the fact that we predicate essential attributes of Him, for in His infinite essence they are all one. It is true that he does not make clear in what way these essential attributes are to be understood; they do not express His essence, for His essence cannot be conceived by us, but nevertheless are positive and essential. It may be that in his insisting that the essence of God is not conceived by us, he means to say that, while these attributes are essential, yet they are not to be understood as final; but our conception of them is incomplete. For instance, we predicate knowledge as an attribute, but we do not know what kind or what degree of knowledge He possesses

---

[94] *Korte Verhandeling*, pp 274-92.   [95] *Ibid.*, p 292

Similarly, Spinoza teaches the infinite perfection of God,[96] and that He possesses infinite attributes,[97] all of which constitute one being. What Spinoza means by attributes was a matter of great controversy, but the interpretation of Fischer [98] is the correct one. According to it, the infinite attributes are infinite forces of God and not different substances. Since the attributes are infinite, it follows that the human mind will never know all of them, and so the essence of God is not conceived fully. The attributes known by us are thought and extension. We see, therefore, that in spite of the widely separating gulf between the two systems, there is still a marked similarity in the basic conception of the attributes. Both teach infinite perfection, infinite unity in spite of the positive content of the attributes, and the incomplete knowledge of the essence. Of course, I am not blind to the differences of their teachings. Spinoza emphasizes that the attributes of extension and thought express the essence of God as forces, and as such are fully conceived by man. Crescas, on the other hand, would shrink in horror from such a conception. But such differences are due to the different nature of Spinoza's system, which is wholly divergent from that of Crescas, as far as the God of a religious man is from the God of a philosopher. Yet they afford points of similarity, especially at the base of their systems where the variance is at its minimum. It can almost be said that Spinoza's system is only a result of carrying out Crescas's principles to their extreme logical conclusion. It will be best illustrated in the chapters on the relation of God and the world, for it is there that the real divergence is evident.

[96] *Epistola XL*

[97] Def 6; *Ethics*, I

[98] K Fischer, *Spinoza*, pp. 380-92.

We see, then, that in spite of Fischer's contention against any possible influence of Crescas on Spinoza there are to be found traces of marked likeness between them. We must not forget that when we say influence we do not mean that the latter actually followed the former, or anything to that effect; what it signifies is a thought impulse and a pointing in a certain direction. That Spinoza read Crescas carefully, and not, as Fischer maintains, was only imperfectly acquainted with him, we have shown above. I wish to remark that Fischer is not entirely just to Crescas by saying of him, 'Denn selbst die Einheit Gottes ist bei ihm kein Object der Erkenntnis, sondern der Offenbarung', and using this fact as an argument to disprove the influence of Crescas on Spinoza. I presume that Fischer means by the words 'die Einheit Gottes' the numerical unity of God, for the essential unity was demonstrated by Crescas as clearly as by Spinoza. But even in regard to the former, it was already mentioned (cp. above) that Crescas's remark in that regard should be taken with reserve, and that it is only a polemic expression. In reality, numerical unity of God is established according to Crescas, since he posits the infinite potence of God. Of course, Spinoza deduces unity with great accuracy from the mere definition of God; but the difference of deduction in the two systems in regard to a certain point does not prove that it is impossible for one system to have influenced the other. It is only religious sufficiency that prevented Crescas from following up his own definition and reaching the same conclusion.

In concluding his theory of attributes Crescas discusses a few emotional qualities which are to be attributed to God. The discussion is interesting, both by the novelty of the

conception, as well as by the interpretations of the emotions.
Aristotle teaches the happiness of God, and deduces it in
the following manner. We must attribute to God the
highest activity which is no higher thing than contemplation,
and since we humans feel pleasure and happiness in thought,
it follows that God who is eternally active, namely contemplative, and the quality of His contemplation being of
the highest and purest kind, must necessarily be always
happy.[99]   Such a conception, says Crescas, is untenable,
and is based on a false theory of emotions. Joy and sorrow,
or pleasure and pain, are contraries, and consequently fall
under the category of action.   They really do not depend
on knowledge, but on will. Pleasure is only the gratification
we derive from the carrying out of our will   Pain, on the
other hand, is the feeling we experience when our will is
obstructed.[100]   If we do experience joy in our knowing,
it is because there is a will to know, and by attaining
knowledge we overcome the obstacle to our will   It will
be evident, therefore, that as far as God is concerned we
cannot attribute any happiness to Him   His knowledge
has no limitations, and there are no obstructions to His
will. When we humans experience any pleasure at conceiving a certain thing, it is because that conception was
not known to us, and in overcoming the obstacle we
experience a sense of pleasure.   But in regard to God
such a mode is inapplicable: whence, then, His happiness
at knowing ?   Crescas asserts, therefore, that if we do

---

[99] *Metaph*, XII, 7, *Ethics*, X

[100] כי השמחה איננה זולת ערבות מהרצון והעצב הוא ההתנגדות ברצון
והם הפעליות נפשיים, *Or Adonai*, p 27 a. Just to know how modern this
theory of emotions is, we have but to compare the views on pleasure and
pain of the English psychologist, E. G Stout, in his *Manual of Psychology*,
chapter on Pain and Pleasure

attribute happiness to God it is because of His love   God is voluntarily the cause of all being, and since we know that existence is goodness, it follows that in so far as God is voluntarily the cause of being, He is voluntarily good. The continuation of the existence of beings is then the continual emanation of His goodness   It is evident, then, that in so far as God continually emanates His goodness and perfection voluntarily, in so far He loves the emanation of goodness necessarily, and it is this action of emanating permeated with love that is described as joy or happiness.[101] This happiness or joy is essential to God, for, as we have seen, it is inherently connected with His being the cause of things and the continual emanation of His goodness and perfection.   We cannot help but express our admiration for such a high ethical conception of the happiness of God, in comparison with which the Aristotelian as well as the Spinozistic (as will be shown) pales as regards the glow of ethical warmth.

In regard to the relations of Crescas and Spinoza on this point of *Amor Dei*, Joel lays great stress on the influence exerted by the former on the latter   The *Amor Dei intellectualis* has two meanings   the love of man towards God, and that of God towards man: but we have to defer the former to a later discussion, where the relation of God and man will be discussed, and occupy ourselves at present with the latter.   Joel contends that Crescas's love of God is not far from the teaching of Spinoza that God loves Himself with an infinite intellectual love.[102]

---

[101] הנה במה שייטפיע מהטוב והשלמות ברצון וכונה הנה א"כ הוא אוהב ההטבה והשפעה הטובה בהכרח והוא האהבה זולת ערבות הרצון, *Or Adonai*, I, 27 a–b.

[102] *Ethics*, V, XXXV, Proposition.

It seems to me that Joel exaggerates a little.   There is, no doubt, a similarity in language, but the content is quite different.   That of Crescas is voluntaristic, that of Spinoza is intellectual in essence.   Pleasure, according to Spinoza, is a transition from a lesser to a greater perfection,[103] and since pleasure is a self-conscious feeling, knowledge necessarily accompanies it.   Again, perfection itself is only knowledge, for, according to the whole Spinozistic system, true ideas have an adequate object, and whatever is false can surely not be perfection   Love is pleasure accompanied by the idea of an external cause.[104]   The external is only necessary as far as human beings are concerned, the idea of cause is the main necessary condition.   It follows, then, that since God is absolutely infinite and necessarily possesses infinite perfection, for reality and perfection are synonymous,[105] He rejoices in that perfection   Furthermore, this rejoicing is accompanied by the idea of Himself, for God possesses that idea,[106] which is the idea of His own being as a cause, and this is what is meant by intellectual love.   We say, therefore, that God loves Himself   But since in God there is not only the idea of His essence, but also of that which follows necessarily from His essence,[107] and under this all beings, and men especially, are meant, it follows that in so far God loves Himself He loves man [108]

We have seen the principal features of this Spinozistic love of God, and it is evident that its content is materially different from that of Crescas   On its emotional and

---

[103] *Ethics*, Part III, Definition of Emotions II.

[104] *Ibid*, Definition of Emotions II

[105] *Ethics*, II, Definition VI.   [106] *Ibid.*, Proposition III

[107] *Ibid.*, Proposition III

[108] *Ethics*, V, Proposition XXXV, Corollary.

formal side it approaches Aristotle's view, which also makes the happiness of God consist in thinking, and Himself the subject of His thoughts. But there is essential difference, this is the idea of cause   It is not the act of thought that makes up the rejoicing, but the being a cause and ground of all being   This is the fundamental difference that widely separates the two conceptions.   On the other hand, it is this same idea of cause that forms a point of contact with Crescas's view.   The latter states that in so far as God is a cause of existence He loves the good, for existence is a continual emanation of good and perfection.   But, again, there is a fundamental difference; Crescas excludes all knowledge from that love. On the other hand, according to Crescas's theory of emotions, which by the way is a very true one, pleasure is not connected with knowledge, but with will.   And also in regard to God's love or happiness he insists on will.   With Spinoza, however, will is entirely omitted, the mechanical or necessary conception takes the ascendancy; knowledge and reality are the principal ingredients in the teaching of Spinoza.

We may, therefore, conclude that while the Crescasian and Spinozistic views on the love of God have a basic point of contact, yet they are totally different in their content, the first is an emotional-voluntaristic, the other a strongly intellectual.   There is a possibility that the term love of God, if not directly borrowed from Crescas, is at least influenced by his use of it, as the term love does not precisely describe the idea which Spinoza wishes to convey by it.   There are some critics who score Spinoza severely for his introducing the conception of *Amor Dei*, and point to the difficulty involved in speaking of God as self-loving, as if He were composed of subject and object.

They assert that the conception is contradictory to the fundamental Spinozistic doctrines.[109]   But this discussion is beyond our point of interest.   The real point of gravity of that question is the *Amor Dei* of man, but this is reserved for the next chapters.   In general, I wish to say that I do not intend to minimize the influence of Crescas upon Spinoza.   On the contrary, I believe that both systems afford many points of contact, and, furthermore, that their source is really one, except that they run in divergent lines. It is possible to find a goodly number of likenesses, but they are never commensurable.   To this point more space will be devoted in the coming chapters.

[109] See K. Fischer in his *Spinoza*, p. 573

PART II

GOD AND THE WORLD

CHAPTER III. INTRODUCTORY.

OPINIONS HELD BY THE PRE-MAIMONIDIAN JEWISH PHILOSOPHERS CONCERNING THE PROBLEMS OF OMNISCIENCE, PROVIDENCE, AND FREEDOM OF THE WILL.

THE problem of the freedom of the will presents one of the most interesting aspects in the history of human thought. Its roots lie far back in antiquity. It arose out of the peculiar position that man holds in the domain of nature, and at the moment that self-consciousness appeared in man and enabled him to reflect upon the surrounding world, and his own personality as related to it Man represents a puzzling riddle unto himself. On the one hand, he feels himself to be the master of things, the lord of being, on the other, contemplation teaches him that he is only a part of that great mysterious environment called nature. Furthermore, this nature is not a haphazard conglomeration of things and events, but there is a kind of succession and sequence, law and order, and to which even he, *nolens volens*, must submit himself. The development of religion simply changed the aspect of the problem It placed man in conflict with the will of the gods, instead of with the blind natural force. With polytheism, however, the gods were not strong enough to replace entirely the

old something that rules over the destiny of man, now
known by the name of fate, and were even themselves
supposed to be dominated by it. Homer says, ' When
the hour of fate comes for man, even a god is helpless, no
matter how much he loves him '.[110] Herodotus goes farther,
and asserts that a God is not able to avoid it.[111] Thus
the problem becomes a much discussed subject in ancient
thought; and it can really be said that out of this dual
character of a man's position there developed Greek ethics
with its special emphasis upon contemplation and thought.

With the rise of monotheism, positing a being all-
powerful, all-wise, and all-knowing, the problem became
more acute. How in the face of such a being, in comparison
with which man dwindles into insignificance, can man save
his personal freedom ? It ought by the nature of the
conception of God to be given up Yet peculiarly enough,
the first monotheistic religion not only did not reject the
freedom of the will, but incorporated it as a dogma.[112]
The story of the receiving of the ten commandments as
described in the Bible,[113] as well as the term covenant used
innumerable times to designate the process of receiving
the Law, implies plainly that man is free and that the
Israelites were entirely at liberty to reject the Law of God.
The idea of freedom is repeated many times in the Bible.[114]
One may argue that the monotheistic conception was
probably loose with the Hebrews in the early times, yet
none can accuse the Hebrew prophets, especially the later
ones, of a lack of pure monotheism, and in spite of it the
freedom of the will is asserted by them with the same

[110] *Iliad*, XVII, 446   [111] Herodotus I, 97
[112] Dr D Neumark, תולדות העיקרים בישראל, I, pp. 81-6.
[113] Exod. 19 10.   [114] Deut 30 19

vigour as the unity of God [115] It is rather a curious fact that the problem of the compatibility of the freedom of the will with that of God's omniscience and providence never found in prophetic writings. There are some usions—in the Psalms—to the problem of injustice, namely, why the righteous suffer and the wicked prosper,[116] and quite a discussion of it in Rabbinic literature,[117] but the problem as a whole was never touched upon.

However, it was bound to crop up. With the rise of scientific philosophic reflection in Judaism, and the manifestation of the desire to base religious dogmas on philosophic principles, the monotheistic conception had to be carried to its logical conclusion, and as a result the problem of the relation of man and God appeared in its full vigour, and demanded a solution. A similar process was going on in the Mohammedan world. The Koran, preaching the purest and most abstract monotheism, and carrying it to logical conclusions, presents a decided predestinarian aspect, though some endeavour to find vestiges of free will in it.[118] But human reason and philosophic speculation felt indignant at such a conception, and revolted against it   This brought about the rise of

[115] Cp. Micah 6 8

[116] Ps 37 25, 26, as well as the contents of the whole chapter, which seems to be intended as an answer to the problem of injustice. The problem itself is stated by Jeremiah in 4 rather bold way when he asks (Jer 12. 1), מדוע דרך רשעים צלחה שלו כל בגדי בגד, also Job grapples with the problem, and cries out, ארץ נתנה ביד רשע פני שופטיה יכסה אם לא אפוא מי הוא 'the earth is given into the hands of the wicked he covereth the face of the judges if not, where and who is he?' (Job 9 24).

[117] Berakot 7 a

[118] Prof. Guyard in his book on 'Abd-er Razzaqu et son traite de la predestination et du libre arbitre', quoted by L. Stein in his *Willensfreiheit*,

P 3

the sects and various doctrines, attempting the solution of the problem in one way or another [119]

The first who dealt with the problem in Jewish philosophy was, as might be expected, Saadia. Saadia says, Man is free in his actions, and there is no intervention on the part of God. This fact is proved by the evidence of sense, of reason, and of tradition We see in daily life that man is master of himself, he speaks or is silent at will, does a number of other things or refrains from doing them, and never conceives that anybody can restrain him in acting according to his wish. This evidence, though it may seem superficial to us, carried a certain amount of conviction to Saadia, who, following the Mutazilites, attached great importance to conception, for whatever can be conceived is real, and the contrary, whatever is not conceived does not possess any reality.[120] Hence the emphasis laid by Saadia on the fact that man conceives and that accordingly he is free. Reason testifies to freedom. First, it is proved that it is impossible for one act to be produced by two agents. If God interfered in human actions, it would be the effect of two agents, God and man. Secondly, if God forces man to do a certain act, what reason would there be for his punishment or reward ? The believer and the atheist would be on an equal footing.[121] As for the

---

[119] ואומר אחרי הדברים האלה כי הבורא אין לו שום הנהנה במעשי בני אדם ואיננו מכריחם לעבודה ולא למרי. ויש לי על זה ראיות מדרך המוחש ומדרך השבל וממה שבכתוב ושבקבלה, *Emunoth Wedeoth*, ed. Josefow, 1885, p 64 b

[120] Cp. Introduction, sect. 3.

[121] *Emunoth Wedeoth*, p 65 a Aristotle offers similar arguments to prove his assertion that man is the originator of things He says: 'Testimony seems to be borne both by private individuals and by lawgivers, too, in that they chastise and punish those that do wrong, while they honour those who

objection on traditional grounds, he quotes a number of verses to that effect.

The problem arises then, How is it possible to conceive freedom of human action and at the same time prescience of God ?   If God knows beforehand that man will rebel against His will, does it not follow *eo ipso* that man must act in this fashion, for otherwise God's knowledge is not perfect ?   Saadia replies that, in reality, the supposed conclusion does not follow.   God's knowledge is not the cause of human actions.   Were it the cause, we should have to grant that man's actions are predestined, for God's knowledge is eternal, and necessarily the effects would be determined, but the case is not so.   It is true that He knows beforehand the events that are going to happen, but He knows them in their true light.   God knows whichever way man is going to select, yet His knowledge does not have any causal relation to the things which are going to happen   It is pure knowledge without any active force. The fact that the things happen in the future and He knows them beforehand does not bear on the subject, for His knowledge is above temporal accidents.   There is only one time existing in regard to God, and that is the present. If one will ask, How is it possible that, if God knows a man is going to speak, yet he could have chosen to be silent ? to this the reply is made, that had he kept silent God's knowledge would have taken cognizance of the fact, for God knows the way man will choose after deliberation.[122]

By way of illustration, we may compare the prescience

---

act rightly '.   Of course, here the reference is not to theological authority, but political , however, the force of the argument is the same   *Nic Ethics*, III, V

[122] *Emunoth Wedeoth*, p 65 a–b

of God, as Saadia conceived it, to a man standing on a very high mountain, and from this exalted position he views an exceptionally long row of men passing by; some have passed, some are passing, and some will pass He sees them all for his position is very elevated, but his seeing is not the cause of their passing [123] However, we cannot help admitting that a shrinkage in God's prescience has been assumed by Saadia. As a result, objections to his theory have been raised by later religious philosophers.[124] But Saadia was very zealous to save human freedom, and some sacrifice had to be made.[125] The problem of the compatibility of the providence of God with the freedom of the will is not treated by Saadia definitely. It seems, nevertheless, from the whole tenor of his book, that he believes in the existence of such a providence, for how could he not believe it? It is found in the Bible. There are, however, some passages bearing on the subject. In one of them it is stated that the events that happen to man are through Divine causality, but at the same time they are partly caused by man himself, namely, that some come as a punishment for his previous choice.[126] The question still remains open. Are the events predestined to happen simultaneously with God's prescience of them, or is it that God causes them to happen after the human actions have taken place? But no such discussion is found

Bahia, as an ethical philosopher, and a man imbued

[123] Commentary to *Emunoth Wedeoth, ad locum*

[124] Albo says that Saadia's view is almost tantamount to the opinion that denies God any knowledge of possibles.

[125] The early Christian fathers encountered a similar difficulty, and followed the same path So did Origen allow a kind of narrowing of God's prescience Fischer, *History of Christian Dogma*, 106

[126] *Emunoth Wedeoth*, 66 b

with religious feeling, does not devote much discussion to this difficult problem in its philosophical aspect. The conflict between freedom and prescience, and the logical contradiction resulting from the full conception of the former, are hardly brought to light The problem is rather viewed from the aspect of Providence He does not call it the problem of freedom and necessity, but of necessity and justice. The point of gravity is, How can we conceive Divine justice in distributing reward and punishment when human actions are pre-ordained? Bahia puts forth several solutions to the problem Some, he says, have denied Providence in regard to human actions, and asserted that man is entirely free, thus saving the justice of God. Some, on the other hand, have given up freedom, but as for justice they denied the possibility of the human understanding to grasp it. Some admit Providence in human actions, excepting such as pertain to right and wrong In such acts choice is left to man. This is really the traditional view expounded in the Talmud.[127] It is also the one that Bahia follows. He feels, however, that the problem is not solved yet, that there are points which demand a solution, especially prescience, this last is not even mentioned by name, but it is surely meant by the following explanation. Just to cover all difficulties, Bahia adds that the ways of God are hidden from man, and human understanding cannot conceive the way God's justice works in the universe.[128] It must be admitted that this solution of the problem is hardly a philosophical one Bahia's distinction between

---

[127] טפה זו מה תהא עליה . . . . ואילו רשע וצדיק לא קאמר כר"ר, Niddah 16 b, also חנינא . . . . הכל בידי שמים חוץ מיראת שמים Berakot 33 b.

[128] *Hobot ha-Lebabot*, pp. 131–32

human and Divine knowledge does not carry with it the speculative characteristics which attend that of Maimonides, who offered a similar suggestion (cp. *infra*). It is simply a blind resignation of a believer to the dogmas of belief.

Halevi treats the problem of freedom in an accurate and philosophical manner. He asserts that human actions are possible and not necessary, and proves it from the general belief of man.[121] Halevi always laid great emphasis on the generality of an idea and the *consensus omnium*. As for the conflict of freedom with God s providence, Halevi evades it by asserting that there are two kinds of Divine causality, direct and indirect. As examples of the first kind may serve such things as the order of the universe, the way and manner of the composition of all living being, the genera of the vegetable kingdom, and all such phenomena that *eo ipso* testify to the plan of a wise maker. As an instance of the second kind, we may quote the burning of a log of wood by fire The immediate cause of this phenomenon is easily explained ; but this cause has another cause, and so on until we finally reach the first cause, still the connexion is not a direct one. We have then a fourfold division of events, divine, natural, chance-wise, and elective or choice-wise.[130] The Divine are those that must be referred immediately to Divine attention, such as have been mentioned The natural arise through mediate causes (סבות אמצעיות), but with an end in view. The chance-wise arise also through mediate causes, but with no particular order or design. The elective are those

---

[121] *Kuzari*, ed Isaac Metz, Hamburg, 1838, p. 119

[130] Corrected by Zifrinowitsch in his edition, p 120, ואם תקצר) תקרב מציאות זה בחלוקה הזאת : המעשים יהיו אלהיים או טבעיים או מקריים או מבחריים Cp for a similar division the *Physics* of Aristotle, II, 5-6

of which the human will is the cause. Freedom is one of
the mediate causes We have then a twofold system
of Divine causality, the immediate and the mediate. The
mediate through the causal nexus returns to God, but
the connexion is a loose one, no force is exerted and man
is free to choose.[181] Divine providence is thus saved, for
all events revert to Him indirectly.   Halevi goes on
polemizing against those that deny the possible. He argues,
If man has no choice in acting, but is forced to perform
the act by the sequence of events, why then do men display
greater anger at the one who injures them willingly than
at the one who does so unwillingly? Are not all human
actions involuntary? [182]

In regard to the problem of the compatibility of the
prescience of God with freedom, Halevi does not add
anything original, but follows Saadia and the Mutazilites,[183]
in asserting that the knowledge of an event beforehand
is not the cause of the realization of that event. Halevi
lays a great deal of stress on the middle causes (cp above).
His ethics thus receives a contemplative aspect. The middle
causes are powerful influences, and it is necessary to know
which to choose and which to obviate.[184] The natural
causes are necessary, but yet there is a possibility by
a knowledge of facts to obstruct their results and avoid
them.   Halevi admits a special kind of Providence, for
in his division of events there is one class of Divine action ,
and there is nothing preventing God from interfering at

---

[181] *Kuzari*, p 120   The idea of the mediate causes was known in
antiquity by the Stoics   Cp L Stein in his *Willensfreiheit*, p 110, note 175

[182] *Kuzari*, p 120

[183] Halevi alludes directly to the Muta'ziliah in that.

[184] *Kuzari*, p. 122

certain occasions, and effecting something immediately
even in a world of mediate causes. He evades however,
the problem of injustice. It is possible, he says, that if we
were able to penetrate and follow up the long series of
causes, we might discover the reasons why the righteous
suffer and the wicked prosper, but this is really beyond
human intelligence. We must, therefore, rely on the
knowledge of God and His justice, and admit our own
shortcomings [135]

Abraham Ibn Daud, the first Aristotelian in Jewish
philosophy, is a strong supporter of the freedom of the
human will. In fact, it is his principal ethical foundation.
He says, Man possesses the possibility to do evil, and the
stronger the inclination is in a certain man, the harder
the struggle to overcome that inclination, the higher the
value which is attached to the virtuous act.[136] He utilizes
the doctrine of the twofold Divine causality, but it is hardly
possible that he borrowed it from Halevi, as he evidently
did not know him.[137] Most likely both derived it from
a common source [138] In regard to the problem of prescience
and freedom, Ibn Daud solves it in a very simple manner.
He concedes that God's foreknowledge is undecided in
regard to the exact way man will act. He knows beforehand that certain actions will be presented to human choice,

---

[135] ואפשר שיגלה בחקירה ברוב הסבות בצדי (בצדיק (Zifrinowitsch
ורע לו רשע וטוב לו ומה שאיננו נגלה ימסרו בו העניין אל דעת האלוהים
וצדקו, p. 125

[136] *Emunah Ramah*, ed. Weil, Frankfurt a M , p 97

[137] In the introduction to the *Emunah Ramah*, p 4, Ibn Daud mentions
that he read Saadia's book as well as Ibn Gabirol, but makes no mention
of the *Kuzari*. This goes to prove that he was unacquainted with it, for
otherwise he certainly would have mentioned it

[138] On this subject there is a difference of opinion between D Kaufmann,
Attributenlehre, p 279, and Stein in his *Willensfreiheit*, p 20, note 43

but not which way he will choose.[139] Ibn Daud is also radical in his theory of Providence. According to him it extends only to the universals, namely, as far as things are connected with the order of the universe, but not to the particulars He, however, excepts the human genus, an exception which we find later in Maimonides. He introduces also an ascending scale of Providence, even in regard to this genus. Those that strive more in the knowledge of God and the principles of reason are especially looked after.[140] The question of the existence of evil in the world is answered by Ibn Daud by negating its reality. There is no evil in the world; God is the cause of good only. The answer is often repeated in Jewish as well as in general philosophy. We shall meet it in a modified form also in Spinoza.

[139] *Emunah Ramah,* p 96

[140] ולעצמים הנכבדים השנחה בנמצאות זה העולם בכללי ובמין האנושי
בפרט והנה על כל פנים ייוחד ההשנחה בשיעור רב אחר זריזותו להפקיד
רוחו אליו, *Ibid ,* p 97

CHAPTER IV

MAIMONIDES' VIEW AND CRESCAS'S COMMENTS

MAIMONIDES, the chief conciliator between theology
and philosophy in Jewish thought, devotes much space
to the elucidation of the problem discussed in the previous
chapter, as well as to its solution in all its aspects
Maimonides, as his predecessors, distinguishes between
the first cause of events and the proximate ones. The
proximate ones he divides, as those before him, into natural,
chance-wise, and choice-wise [141]   Choice, however, is the
exclusive gift of man who is endowed with a special faculty.
Maimonides introduces a distinction, already made by
Aristotle,[142] between instinctive willing which is only
a result of desire, and human choice.[143]   He, however,
does not connect choice with reason as much as Aristotle
does   Maimonides, as a theologian, attributes it to a direct
act of the will of God.   Just as God willed that fire should
tend upwards and earth downwards, so did He institute
that man should be master of himself, and his actions
should be in his own hands.[144]   He, like Ibn Daud,

[141] *Moreh*, II, ch. 48 , *Guide*, p 222.

[142] Moral choice is plainly voluntary, but the two are not coextensive,
voluntary being the more comprehensive term ; for first, children and all
other animals share in voluntary action, but not in moral choice   *Ethics*,
III, 2 113 b

[143] ור"ל בבחירה שהיה סבת המתחדש ההוא בחירת אדם עד שאפילו
היתה הסבה רצון אחד משאר בעלי חיים, *Moreh*, II, ch. 48.   Notice the
distinction between בחירת אדם and רצון בעלי חיים.

[144] Code, Div 1, Teshubah (Penitence , ch 5, 4 ; *Guide*, III, 8

recognizes the inclination in man to do evil, and therefoie
assumes freedom as a standard of actions; the moie the
stiuggle, the highei the worth of the ethical action   Since
free will was instituted in man by the will of God, it may
on special occasion be taken away fiom man, such as we
find in the case of Pharaoh [145]   This case is well known to
all theological philosophers, Christian as well as Jewish.[146]
Of course, such a possible limitation will not be pleasing
to the upholdei of absolute free will.

In regard to the Divine knowledge, Maimonides, after
polemizing against some of the philosophers who wanted
to limit it, asserts that God is omniscient and nothing is
hidden from Him.[147]   In this connexion, Maimonides
remarks that gieat philosophers of the pre-Aristotelian
period accepted the doctrine of omniscience.   He refers
to the book *De Regimine,* by Alexander of Aphrodisias,
wheie their opinions are quoted.   The only one to whose
opinion we find a distinct reference is Sociates.   In
Xenophon's *Memorabilia* he is quoted as preaching that
the gods know all things, what is said, what is done, and
what is meditated in silence.[148]   Maimonides further asserts
that this knowledge is eternal.   The problem then appears
in full vigour, How are we to reconcile the freedom of
man with this prescience?   The answer to this problem
Maimonides finds in his Theory of Attributes (cp above) [149]
Maimonides conceives the Divine attiibutes in a negative
way, and says that when applying the same attiibutes to
God and man, we use them in an absolute homonymous

[145] Chapters of Maimonides, ch 8, ref. to Exod 7 3
[146] Origen, *De Principiis,* III, 1, grapples with this problem.
[147] *Guide,* III, 16.   [148] *Memorabilia,* I, 1. 19
[149] Chapter 2

way. This theory contends that it is absolutely impossible
for the human mind to grasp the meaning of the attributes
applied to God. Since the attribute of prescience forms
no exception, the difficulty is solved   The problem arises
only when we conceive knowledge in the human sense.
With man, knowledge is correlative with fact. Applying
the same conception by analogy to that of God, it follows
that God's prescience ought to agree with the fact, otherwise
it contradicts itself   But since we do away with that
analogy and assert that His knowledge is different in kind,
the difficulty disappears.   God knows things beforehand,
yet the possible still remains.[150]   This teaching is not
merely a concession of ignorance, but, as mentioned,
grounded in the theory of attributes.   God's knowledge
is not a separate thing from His essence but connected
with it, and just as the essence, it is unknown.   In the act
of human knowledge we distinguish the יודע ידוע מדע, the
knower, the known, and the knowledge itself, but with God
He is all three in one [151]

As for the question of Providence, Maimonides treats
it in detail   He quotes four different opinions, and then
adds his.   The first is the Epicurean, denying Providence
entirely.   The second is the Aristotelian, in the garb of
Alexander of Aphrodisias,[152] namely, that Divine providence
ceases at the sublunar world.   But as Providence, even
in regard to the spheres, consists mainly in their preserva-

[150] *Guide*, III, ch 20

[151] Chapters 1–8   A similar use of the homonymous theory is made by
Spinoza, *Cogitata Metaph.*, VI, 9   It is interesting to compare with the last
Fischer's note 24 in his *Anhang* to Spinoza.

[152] As for Aristotle himself, it is doubtful whether he ever expressed any
opinion on the subject   See Jules Le Simon in his *Étude de la Théodicée de
Platon et Aristote*, p 100 f

tion, it filtrates also to a certain degree to the sublunar world, in so far as the genera are endowed with perpetual preservation. The third is that of the Ash'aria—extremists on the orthodox side of the Kalamitic movement—assuming perfect subjection of the universe and its beings to the Divine will, denying chance and choice. The fourth is that of the Mutazilites, positing freedom, and Divine justice and Providence at the same time. They went so far in their conception of justice, according to Maimonides, that they extended reward even to animals for their being killed.[153] The fifth is his own, which according to him agrees with the Jewish tradition. Divine providence extends in the sublunar world to the human species only The other beings are subjected to chance or natural law. However, he admits that the genera of other beings have a kind of providence in so far as the natural law originates from God.[154] As it is evident, the Maimonidian theory differs from the so-called Aristotelian only in attributing Providence to the human species. The reason for the exception is found in the possession by the human genus of the mind, which is a means of conveyance for Divine emanation It follows, therefore, as we noticed in Ibn Daud, that the one who is more intellectually perfect should receive more attention from Providence [155]

Note —Objections to this last assertion have been raised by many religious thinkers, and with justice Among the thinkers is also the Karaite Aaron Ben Elijah in Eṣ Ḥayim.

---

[153] והוא שאני אאמין שההשגחה האלהית אמנם היא בזה העולם התחתון ר"ל מתחת נלגל הירח באישי מין האדם לבד, *Moreh*, ch. 17.

[154] *Guide*, III, ch. 17. For a certain inadequateness in his exposition of the Mutazilistic teaching see Stein, *Die Willensfreiheit*, p. 86.

[155] *Guide*, III, 17, 18.

W.   H

The chief critic, however, is Crescas himself. This question will be discussed in detail. I have also omitted for the present the Maimonidian theory of origin of evil, as well as some philosophic arguments for the denial of prescience and Providence quoted by Maimonides. These are discussed at length by Crescas, and should be taken in connexion with his own solutions as they form a part of his theory.

CRESCAS ON PRESCIENCE

Crescas, as a foundation to his discourse on the subject, posits three principles, which, according to him, agree with and are necessitated by tradition. These are (a) the infinite science of God, (b) His prescience, (c) that His foreknowledge of the possible event does not change the nature of it. He proceeds then to analyse the philosophical doubts that arise in connexion with such conceptions, and, as usual, reproduces them first. First, if God knows the events happening in this world, it follows that God is being perfected by this knowledge, for it has been established that knowledge is a kind of perfection, but such conclusion is absurd, for how can the absolute Perfect be perfected through the knowledge of inferior things? Second, since it is known that the mind in conceiving things becomes identified with the concepts and assimilates them to its essence, it follows that there will result a multiplicity in God's essence, for the things are many. The third and fourth arguments attack God's assumed knowledge of particulars. There were two current philosophical opinions in regard to the Aristotelian conception of the matter. The first denied entirely God's knowledge of anything external to Himself. (This seems to be the right one, cf. above, Introduction, IV.) The other, following Alexander, admitted the knowledge of universals [156] Particular things can be conceived only through their matter and passive intellect, but God has no matter; it follows that He cannot conceive the particular things.[157] Again, particulars are temporal, and whatever relates to time is an accident of motion ; but God is above motion and time, He therefore does not know of the particulars. Finally, the positing of Divine science of the world's affairs is untenable, as the disorder in the natural sphere and the existence of evil in human affairs testify [158]

These are the objections to the general principle of positing God's knowledge of the world's affairs.   There are several objections especially to several of the specific principles, namely, the infinite science of God and His pre-science.   How, asks the opponent, can God's knowledge be infinite? Is not knowledge a comprehensive and determining thing ?   How, then, can the infinite be comprehended or determined ? There is then a contradiction in terms   Again, prescience seems to be impossible. Real knowledge of a thing implies that the object known exists, for in what consists

[156] Gersonides, *Milḥamot*, III, 1, p 120.

[157] All these objections are also found arranged in a similar order in Gersonides, *Milḥamot*, III, 2 However, we notice in Crescas a more logical arrangement It is not necessary that he borrowed them directly from Gersonides, though the contents and form are similar. These objections were current in the thought of the age   Some of them are also mentioned by Maimonides In the third objection there is a digression by Crescas which deserves some notice. It is the first with Gersonides He says that the particular is conceived through the hylean power such as sense and imagination Crescas substitutes matter instead of sense. That would agree with the Aristotelian conception of individuality which consists in matter, for it is this that gives the uniqueness since form is general to genus. *Metaph.*, XII, 8

[158] *Or Adonai*, p 29 a.

the truthfulness of a conception of things if not in the fact
that the mental conception of a thing agrees with the object
existing outside of the mind ? [159]   Furthermore, if we grant
that God does know things before their occurrence, a change
in His knowledge is necessitated.   Before they occur He
knows them as future happenings, after that as past.   And
since the mind essence changes with the concepts, there
will then be a change in His essence, but this is impossible
The assumption that the existence of possible future events
is compatible with the prescience of God is also assailed.
If we posit that God knows before the realization of one
of the two possible aspects of a future event, and at the
same time we assert that the opposite aspect is possible
of occurrence; then while in His prescience the opposite
is still conceived as possible, after the action occurs the
possibility is removed and a change in the Divine knowledge
necessarily effected.   Moreover, the assumption that God
knows whichever aspect is going to occur proves to be
untenable, for with a possible event, in as far as it is
possible, either side may be assumed.   Suppose, then,
that we assume the opposite side of that of which God is
prescient, existing, if so absurdities would result, (a) a change
in His knowledge, (b) a falsity in it   If that cannot be the
case, the possible is done away with and God's prescience
involves the necessity of human actions.[160]

After reproducing at length all the objections, which,
as remarked, are identical with those quoted by Gersonides
in his book *Milhamot* (The Battles of the Lord), Crescas
quotes also the Gersonidian solution, though not mentioning

[159] Cp Locke's definition of knowledge in *Essay on Human Understanding*,
Bk. 4, ch 1.
[160] *Or Adonai*, Tr. II, p 29 a

him by name. The objection may be answered in the
following manner. The first which involves the question
of God's perfection disappears when we consider that the
existence of other beings arises through God's existence,
and also conceived through His own conceptions. His
knowing other beings would not mean then an additional
perfection, for He knows them through the general order
of things (סדור הכולל), the principle of which is in Himself.[161]
The second, raising the objection of multiplicity, is solved
by the same conception. Since God knows the general
order which emanates from Himself, and this order unites
all the different things (for though things are different in
certain respects they are also connected in a certain aspect
and perfect each other), He then knows the particulars from
their side of unity. In the same manner the third doubt
is refuted. It is founded on the principle that in order
to know the particulars God must possess hylic powers,
but though we grant the validity of the principle it does
not follow that God should not know the particular things
through their general conceived order wherein their unity
is manifested. The doctrine of the inherence of things in
the general order also meets the fourth objection, basing
itself on the fact that particulars are in time, while God,
is above time, for God's conception of the general order
does not depend upon time. The fifth, the question of
evil, is deferred for future discussion Again, the other
doubts, named by Crescas partial, are also met. The
difficulty of knowledge being infinite (cp. above), it is done
away with by removing the infinite. Things are infinite
in their differentiation but not in their unity.[162] The

---

[161] *Milḥamot*, III, 4 , *Or Adonai*, p 29 b.

[162] The words in the text, both in Gersonides and Crescas, are סדור מושכל,

general order preconceived by God is finite.   In the same
way the two objections raised against prescience (cp. above)
are righted   Since God knows things through their general
order which emanates directly from Him, the things are
already existing, and surely there is no change in the
knowledge itself   If God knew the particulars in as far as
they are particulars, that is from the point of their differentiation, that change would be implied, but He knows
them from their general order, and this is not changed.
Finally, the most difficult question is solved; this is the
question of the existence of the possible in spite of
prescience   Possible events have two aspects, and may
be preordained in one way, and possible in the other.
From the aspect of general order of events they are
determined, but from the aspect of human choice they
are indeterminate   God knows these things only so far
as they are possible, but He does not know which side
of the possibility will be realized.   It is evident, therefore,
that when Gersonides speaks of possible things as being
determined by the general order, he means that only their
possibility is determined but not their realization.[163]

Crescas, in resuming the foregoing discussion, points
out that the reasoning of those philosophers—still not
mentioning any name—compel us to posit two principles:
(1) God knows the particulars only through their general
order , (2) God knows only that certain things are possible,
but not the manner of their realization   From these two
conceptions there follows necessarily a third one.   God
does not know of the happenings of one of the possible

which means literally conceived arrangement, i. e division into genera.
But the concept of genus implies always the notion of unity.

[163] *Milḥamot*, III, 4 , *Or Adonai*, pp. 29 b–30 a.

sides, even *a posteriori*.[164]   Were He to know of the fact,
a change in His knowledge would be implied.   Before the
occurrence of the event He knew of it only as a possible,
and after it as actual.   Crescas sees in such an assumption
a shrinkage of God's science, a dangerous doctrine, and sets
out in his acute manner to refute it.   These philosophers,
he says, have not solved the doubts at all.   In spite of
their insisting on unity by positing that God knows things
through the unified aspect, namely, the general order, these
philosophers, according to Crescas, have not succeeded in
removing multiplicity.   True knowledge consists in knowing
things through all their causes, mediate or immediate
Knowledge of composed things then would be perfect only
when the elements of which they are composed would be
conceived by the knower, for the elements are causes
of things, but the elements are many, there follows then
that the knower must conceive the manifold.   Again, even
if we grant that existing things form a kind of unified order
of perfection, this will be true only of the broadest genera,
such as the division of the kingdoms, e. g. the vegetative,
animal, &c., but considering the narrower genera or the
species, we find that one does not perfect the other, e. g.
the horse has no relation of perfection to the donkey.
If we posit, then, of God a knowledge of genera, He cannot
escape conceiving multiplicity   Thirdly, even if we assume
that God's knowledge is limited to the spheres and intelligibles, the difficulty is not solved, for though they
present a certain unity they also exhibit differentiation;
the knowledge of the differentiating aspect would then

---

[164] ויתחיב להם ענין ג' וזה שאחר שיניע חחלק האחד מחלקי האפשר
אין לו ידיעה בו, *Or Adonai*, p. 30 a

imply multiplicity.[165]   Lastly, there is an astrological
argument directed chiefly against Gersonides, who attributes great influence to the spheres and constellations
The knowledge of particulars by God arises, according to
him, out of the order of the heavenly spheres, which order
is due to the various combinations of the constellations
But the combinations may be infinite, for the great circle
in the sphere is a quantity, and it is infinitely divisible.
It follows, then, that the arrangements can be infinite, and
so God's science does not escape multiplicity

It is evident, then, that the principal object in removing
the manifold from Divine knowledge has not been obtained.
But there is still a greater error   The followers of the
foregoing theory, in their endeavours to put forth an exalted
conception of God, have attributed to Him imperfections,
namely, finiteness. If, as they say, God does not know
the particulars as particulars, it follows, since the number
of particular things is infinite, that He possesses ignorance
in regard to the infinite, and that the relation of God's
knowledge to His ignorance is as the finite to the infinite,
for the number of things that He does know is finite.
Again, if God does not know beforehand which of the two
possible sides of an event will be realized, it appears, since
the possible events are incomparably greater than the
necessary ones, that God is ignorant of most of the happenings of the world.   Lastly, those philosophers, in order
to avoid the assumption of the possibility of a change in
God's knowledge, asserted that God does not know of the

[165] והג' בשהונחה הידיעה מצד הסדור הכולל בגרמים השמימיים
ובשכלים הנפרדים שאישיהם נצחיי באיש והם מתחלפים במין הנה בצד
אשר הם מתחלפים במין אינם מתאחדים הידיעה א"כ בהתחלף עצמיהם
במין כבר תחיב רבוי ידועים, *Or Adonai*, p 30b

result of a possible happening, even as a past occurrence.
If this is the case, we must evidently assume that God is
ignorant of the greatest part of human history, for in the
long row of centuries thousands of possible actions, events,
and occurrences were realized, and all these things escaped
His knowledge; such an assertion is certainly absurd [168]

To meet all these doubts and objections, Maimonides
put up his theory of the homonymity of the Divine attributes. (See above in the exposition of the Maimonidian
theory.) This theory was severely attacked by Gersonides
He argues that it is impossible to speak of absolute
homonymity in regard to Divine attributes   In attributing
to God certain qualities, and speaking of them as belonging
to Him, we inevitably borrow human conceptions.   The
case in question furnishes an example.   We conceive
knowledge as a perfection, we attribute it also to God.
But in this case no absolute homonymy is possible, for
when one attribute is predicated of two things, it is impossible to be used in an homonymous way, as it does not
then convey the same idea   Again, when we negate certain
attributes in regard to God, we do not negate them in an
homonymous way.   When we say, God is not movable,
we do not mean that His not being moved and the not
being moved of a certain thing are absolutely homonymous,
for in this case the idea that we wish to convey is not at all
proved.   He may be moved, and yet the movement has
no association with what we call being moved.   Still we
go on negating.   Again, if all attributes are employed
in an homonymous way, why shall we not say, God is
a body, conceiving it in an absolute homonymous way with
no relation to what we call body?   Gersonides, therefore,

assumes that all attributes and knowledge included are said to differ in their application to God and man only in degree, but not in kind. The Maimonidian solution of the problem of prescience and the possible falls then, the foundation being undermined [167]

Against the assailment of Gersonides, Crescas steps forth as a defender of Maimonides. Knowledge attributed to God and man must be in an absolute homonymous way. It cannot be said that it differs only in degree, for the content of any attribute predicated of things and differing in degree, is the same, no matter how widely the degrees it may connote in various applications may differ, as, for instance, the content of existence, which is predicated of substance as well as of other things.[168] The contents in both predications are the same, namely being, but the degrees are various, substance exists through itself, while the other things exist through the substance. But in speaking of the knowledge of God, since His knowledge is a kind of essential thing, and His essence is different from ours in kind, it follows that the same will be said of His knowledge. It is true that negatively, when conceiving the attributes under a negative aspect, namely knowledge, denoting not ignorant, existent, not non-existent, the contents are one when employed of God and man. But when applying these attributes in a positive way, we must admit that the application is homonymous. It is evident from the exposition, and more so on reading the original, that Crescas finds himself in his defence in a rather difficult position.

[167] *Milhamot*, III, 3

[168] The word in the text is מאמרות, which means literally Categories, but to one who is not acquainted with the Aristotelian conception of Categories the word here would be confusing.

He apparently contradicts himself in defending Maimonides, and in assuming the homonymy theory he changes his own attitude which he expressed in his first section,[169] where he distinctly states that existence, when applied to God and man, is not used absolutely homonymously, but in a kind of non-essential likeness,[170] and he speaks definitely of a difference in degree. However, the contradiction is removed by his insisting on the distinction between a negative proposition and a positive, and claiming that while the negative content may have a likeness, the positive which we are going to assume may differ absolutely. Still, Crescas admits that it is only defensive, but he himself probably holds a different view. Towards the end of the argument he remarks 'Be it whichever way, whether following the master (Maimonides) that knowledge is applied homonymously or that there is only a difference of degree as we say, and denotes an essential attribute as we showed in the third section of the first tractate, it remains for us to solve the question in a different way '[171]

Crescas then proceeds to state his own view. The real and special distinction between the knowledge of God and ours is that His knowledge is active and causal, and ours derivative. Through His knowledge and true plan of His will, the known existing things have acquired their existence. Our knowledge is derived from the existing

---

[169] See *Or Adonai*, I, sect iii, p. 22 a, and *supra*, ch II, 2

[170] The Hebrew word is סְפּוּק, which is to be translated by the whole phrase, cp Maimonides, מלות ההגיון, p 43

[171] ואיך שיהיה משם היריעה אם שיהיה בשתוף גמור כדרך הרב אם שיאמר בקדימה ואיחור ויורה על תואר עצמותו במו שנראה אנחנו למה שהידיעה תהיה לעצמותו כמו שקדם לנו בכלל הג' מהמאמר הא' וכבר נשאר עלינו שנאמר בהתר הספקות בדרך מיוחד מה שיספיק בו כמו שיערנו, *Or Adonai*, p. 32 b

things by means of the senses and imagination.[172] This
fundamental difference will remove all objections. First,
in regard to God it cannot be said that knowledge of
external things adds perfection, for it is this knowledge that
causes the existence of other things. It is evident, therefore, that the things themselves cannot add anything to their
cause since they are dependent upon it. The difference
between Crescas's point of view and that of Gersonides
must be made clear at the outset, as the solution of the
first objection by Gersonides seems to be similar in
language.[173] Gersonides also speaks of the fact that the
existence of other things is dependent upon the existence
of God, and that God's conception of other things is derived
through the conception of His self. The difference consists
in this, that Gersonides left out the voluntary element; the
God of Gersonides, as well as of some others of the Peripatetic followers, was to a certain degree an imperfect
personality. God, they say, is the cause of existence, but
not directly, only through a kind of emanation by means
of certain emanative beings which form a channel of
causality. He knows the beings by knowing Himself, but
He knows them only by means of the general order;
the details were left to the other emanated beings. It is
this loophole that enabled Crescas to overthrow the whole
Gersonidian structure, and show its logical unsoundness
(see his argument above). The great failure of the Peripatetic philosophical theologians was that they stopped
midway between an absolute personality of God and an

[172] שההפרש המיוחד בין ידיעתו לידיעתנו . . . . שמידיעתו וציור רצונו
קנו הידועים המציאות. וידיעתנו אצולה וקנויה מהידועים באמצעות החוש
הרמיון, *Or Adonai*, p 32 b

[173] *Milhamot*, III, 2, and exposition above.

absolute impersonality. Spinoza followed the last path, and arrived at his system where God is not only the cause of the world but also the ground, Crescas the first; and both of them succeeded in a certain way. Moreover, several of their conclusions are strikingly similar, for the principle is really one, a certain wholeness, but of this further. Crescas conceives the beings as arising not through emanation, but through the will and plan of God, and as every plan requires preceding knowledge; God's knowledge of things therefore is causal, nay, it is creative. He knows things, not because He knows Himself, but *eo ipso*; it is through His knowledge that they exist. This knowledge and will are not to be construed in any gross form, but, as has been discussed, they are essential attributes The second objection disappears also, for there is no multiplicity implied on account of the fact that the known things are many and the mind assimilates and identifies itself with the things known. This objection may be true of a derivative mind, but not of God who is the cause of the existence of things, and thus knows them whether one or many.

In this way, God also knows the particulars without using the senses and imagination as a means of conception, for the particular also acquires its existence through His knowledge. The question of time, which is raised by the fourth objection, namely, that particulars are in time, is removed, for even time derives its existence from Him. Besides, Crescas has already shown (above, chapter I) that time is not an accident of motion but a mental concept The argument from the existence of evil in this world is deferred for a later chapter.[174]

[174] *Or Adonai*, p 32 b.

Crescas then proceeds to discuss the objections which he terms partial. The question, How can knowledge comprehend an infinite number of things? is answered by maintaining that the objection would be valid if the knowledge were of a finite kind such as the human is, but since it is itself infinite there is no difficulty. The contention that God's knowledge may be infinite is strictly connected with the possibility of the existence of an infinite number of effects, and this is maintained by Crescas (cp. above, chapter I of this work). The second argument insisting that foreknowledge of a thing implies already the existence of the thing known, for it is this that constitutes true knowledge, is met by Crescas in the following manner. The assertion, he says, is true of human knowledge which is derivative, but not of God's; His prescience of a thing that it will exist is real and true, for it is that which assures the thing its existence. The other difficulty connected with the question of prescience, the one of change, namely, that there is a change in the status of the thing from being a future happening to a past occurrence, and therefore also a change in the knowledge of it, does not affect the knowledge of God, for He knows beforehand that at a certain time the event will happen   He finally arrives at the most difficult part of the problem, the compatibility of the existence of the possible with God's prescience. How can we call a thing possible when God knows beforehand whichever way it is going to happen?   Here Crescas gives us a glimpse of his theory of an apparent or nominal possible. His consistency in refusing to admit any shrinkage in God's prescience forces him to abandon a great part of the freedom of the will. A thing, he says, may be necessary in one way and possible in another.[175] As an example he cites the knowledge which a man has of certain things that are possible of existence, as most things are   The knowledge that we have of them necessitates their existing, for knowledge is an agreement of the mental ideas with the things existing.   Yet this knowledge does not change their nature of being possible of existence. In a similar way, the knowledge of God knowing the way which man will elect does not change the nature of the possibility   It must be admitted that the example is not happily chosen, for human knowledge of things is *a posteriori*, the possibility of the existence is already a past thing, while the knowledge of God which we speak of is *a priori*, and the possibility is still existing.   In addition, human knowledge is not causal, while that of God is, and His prescience must affect the future occurrence, unless we assume with Saadia that God's knowledge is not the cause of things ; but Crescas really argued the contrary.   However, the question is taken up again in connexion with freedom of the will, and he solves it quite dexterously.

It is a mooted question whether Spinoza's reputed impersonality of God is so complete as many of his interpreters want to attribute to him [176]   There are others who assert that in spite of some passages which lend themselves to such an interpretation, the God of Spinoza is not entirely robbed of consciousness.[177]   The question what Spinoza meant by God's knowledge or intellect is dependent on the previous conception.   The language is confusing, and

[175] והנה יתבאר לה במה שאומר אין ספק שהיות הדבר מחויב בצד מה לא יחיב חיוב הדבר בעצמותו, *Or Adonai*, p 33 a

[176] Cp K Fischer, *Spinoza*, p. 366.

[177] Joel, *Zur Genesis der Lehre Spinozas*, p. 16

the passages often ambiguous. It seems, however, that a certain discrepancy exists between his earlier remarks on the subject of Divine knowledge in the *Cogitata Metaphysica* and that of the *Ethics*. In the former, his language is more in accord with the philosophico-theological terms. He attributes omniscience to God, and of singulars more than of universals In his polemics against those that want to exclude singulars from God's science, he reminds us of Maimonides in denying any existence to universals.[178] He further speaks of God being the object of His own thoughts. In the *Ethics*, on the other hand, in the famous scholium to proposition XVII in the first book of *Ethics*, Spinoza remarks, ' that neither intellect nor will appertain to God's nature', yet again, in the same scholium he describes the way he attributes intellect and will to God in quite Maimonidian fashion, insisting on absolute homonymy in applying these attributes to God. Again, in a corollary to proposition XXXII, in the first book, Spinoza says: ' Will and intellect stand in the same relation to the nature of God as do motion and rest and absolutely all natural phenomena.' This last passage shows Spinoza's view of God to be impersonal; yet he goes on to say in the scholium to proposition VII, book II, that 'whatsoever can be perceived by the infinite intellect as constituting the essence of substance belongs altogether to one substance'. What the word 'perceived' means here is difficult to tell. Joel concludes that all that Spinoza means to say in the scholium is that there is no relation between the human

---

[178] Cp Maimonides, *Guide*, III, 18, and *Cogitata Metaph*, pt II, ch 7 : ' deinde res realiter existentes Deum ignorare statuunt universalium autem, quae non sunt nec ullam habent praeter singularium essentiam, cognitionem Deo affingunt '.

conception of these attributes and their real nature as they exist in God.[179]   His conclusion, however, may be un-justified, but the discussion is beyond the range of our work

What interests us most are two points, which bear a decided resemblance to the theory of Crescas.   Spinoza speaks of the intellect of God as the cause of things both in regard to their essence and their existence [180]   Things arise because they exist by representation as such in the intellect of God.   It is not clear what Spinoza may mean by 'representation'.   To take it literally would mean a too great concession to personality, but whatever it intended to convey, even if we grant that it may connote the necessity of the unfolding of the attribute of thought, the formal side of it is almost identical with the teaching of Crescas, which, as was shown, emphasizes the point that the knowledge of God is the cause of things not only through the general order, but of the essence of all things.   Again, Spinoza repeats continually that the intellect and the will of God are identical.[181]   It is exactly the same teaching that we find in Crescas when he says that 'through His knowledge and representation of His will the things acquired existence'.[182]   Such a conception is necessitated when knowledge is conceived as an efficient cause, not merely contemplation as Aristotle conceives the Divine thought to be.   It is true that there may be a difference of contents in these two conceptions, that of Crescas having a voluntaristic ring, while that of Spinoza

---

[179] *Zur Genesis der Lehre Spinozas*, p 18
[180] *Ethics*, Bk I, Prop 17, scholium
[181] *Ethics*, Prop 17, scholium, p 32.
[182] *Or Adonai*, p 32 b

a ground of causal necessity, but still the kinship of the teachings cannot be denied. It is not definitely known whom Spinoza had in mind when he makes the statement in connexion with the intellect of God in the foregoing passage, ' This seems to have been recognized by those who have asserted that God's intellect, God's will, and God's power are one and the same'; but that in Crescas this idea is expressed clearly is evident However, we shall return to this subject later in the discussion on will and creation.

I wish, nevertheless, to say a few words concerning K. Fischer's stand on the subject. Spinoza, in scholium to proposition VII, book II of his *Ethics*, in discussing the unity of thinking and extended substance, remarks ' This truth seems to have been dimly recognized by those Jews who maintained that God, God's intellect, and the things understood by God are identical '. Fischer, in quoting this passage,[183] does not attach much importance to any influence which it may possibly indicate, but in note 34 in his *Anhang* he says : ' Derartige Vorahnungen einer Identitatsphilosophie finden sich nicht wie man gemeint hat bei Maimonides, sondern bei Ibn Esra, so in dessen beruhmtem Satz (Exod. 24), כי הוא לבדו יודע ורעת (He alone is knower, knowledge, and known)'. Why Fischer should see in this dictum the foreshadowing of the Spinozistic identity of substances is difficult to see, as well as his discovery of it in Ibn Ezra alone. This identical dictum is quoted also by Maimonides in the eighth chapter of his treatise known as ' The Eight Chapters ', where he says . ' It has been explained that He, blessed be His name, is His attributes, and His attributes are He, so that it is said of Him that He is the knowledge, the knower, and the

[183] *Spinoza,* p 273

known, He is life, living, and the cause of His own life'. It was also quoted quite often by the Arabic philosophers This dictum does not contain any other idea than the Aristotelian conception that God is the object of His own thought, and it is quoted by Maimonides in this sense to show the difference between God's knowledge and that of man, which is something separate from the subject, the knower. The later commentators of Aristotle interpreted Aristotle to mean that God in thinking of His own subject conceives ideas which are realized in the world as general principles, and so He knows the universals. It is in this sense that it was used by Ibn Ezra, following the Arabic philosophers who maintained that God's science is only limited to general order, but no foreshadowing of Spinoza can be seen in that dictum. If any claim to foreshadowing is admitted on that basis alone, Maimonides surely cannot be excluded from being a forerunner of Spinoza, as has been shown That the origin of the dictum is to be found in the Aristotelian conception of God's thinking quoted in *Metaphysics*, XII, 7 and 9, has been pointed out by L. Stein [184] Vestiges of a Spinozistic identity conception can be found only in Crescas, but of that later.

[184] *Willensfreiheit*, pp 70, 116

CHAPTER V

PROVIDENCE, POTENCE, AND FREE WILL

CRESCAS posits that the providence of God extends
also to particulars, yet it is not entirely uniform. It
presents rather a kind of graded scale. It is in some
aspects generic and universal, and in some way individual.
The general is again subdivided into a more general order
where the system is natural law without any particular
attention to the perfection of the species or individual
included, and into a special kind where the perfection
of the unit is in some way taken into consideration.
Again, the individual providence, though not in the form
of natural law and a kind of special, yet admits of division.
There is some kind in which the perfection of the provided
individuals is completely taken into view, and some kind
in which the relation of Providence to the provided is not
so absolute in regard to their perfection. Crescas goes
on to exemplify his division. The general Providence is
seen in every existing being, in its composition, natural
tendencies, organic functions, mental powers, and so forth.
Although these forces vary according to the genus and the
species, they are alike in every individual of the species;
we see, therefore, that natural laws are taken in as a part
of Providence. The human species is an example of general

and special Providence, since it is endowed with reason.
It is general, for every individual participates in it alike,
but special at the same time as it is only for that species
alone. Thus he goes on to unnecessary details. The
particular Providence, in his conception, consists in the
spiritual reward and punishment, for the following of an
ethical and religious life or the opposite. This kind of
Providence is in complete relation to the degrees of perfection of the various individuals, and it is arranged and
determined by God's eternal will [185] We observe here
already a departure from the theories of the Jewish
Aristotelians who emphasized the intellect as a means for
special providence,[186] and asserted that the higher man
ascends in the scale of intelligence the greater claim he
has upon God's special interest. Crescas, on the other
hand, asserts the practical and ethical value over the
intellectual.[187]

The problem of injustice in this world is taken up next
by Crescas. It was always a stumbling-block to religious
thinkers, and various solutions have been offered for its
removal. Of these Crescas quotes several. The first is the
Maimonidian, which denies the existence of the problem
either by doubting the subject, namely, whether the righteous
is really righteous or only apparently so, or by questioning
the predicate, saying that the evil of the righteous is for
the purpose of the good, and the good of the wicked for
the purpose of evil.[188] Both possibilities are objected to

[185] והוא מבואר היות ההשגחה הזאת מסודרת ומוגבל ברצונו הקדום,
Or Adonai, p. 35 a   קדום here is to be taken rather as eternal than predestined. Crescas uses the word often in the sense of eternal

[188] See above, chapter III   Ibn Daud, and cp also Maimonides on this
point

[187] Or Adonai, p 35 a.   [188] Ibid., p 35 b.

by Crescas.   The fact is that we observe at times that
evil befalls a man when he acts righteously, and again when
the same man turns to the wrong path he succeeds.   This
turn of events gives the case a problematic status, for
whatever the man really is, not apparently, the results
ought at least to follow in opposite directions.   On the
other hand, the denial of the predicate is contravened by
fact, for we find many evils that befall the righteous with
no purpose for the good, and the opposite.

Again, the solution of the quasi-Aristotelians, which
is rather Neo-Platonic, that evil has its origin in matter
and has little to do with God, is not satisfactory, for that
simply leads to admit a shrinkage of God's power.
Gersonides tried to solve this question in a peculiar
manner.[189] Providence follows the intellectual scale   Man
through his reason and potential unity with the active
reason stands in a certain relation to God   The more man
develops his mental powers the nearer he comes to God,
and so is said to be under special Providence.   On the
other hand, the one that neglects the cultivation of
the intellect is forsaken.   The purpose of the special
Providence is to provide the deserving with adequate
causes to obtain the good.   However, exceptions to the
rule occur very often, and the cause of these exceptions
is the influence of the spheres.   The wicked sometimes
prosper because of a certain sidereal arrangement.   Again,
the suffering of the righteous may be explained through
other causes also.   As for the influence of the spheres,
though in particular cases it may be unjust, yet taken as
a whole it tends for the good, preservation of the existence,

---

[189] Crescas refers to Gersonides by the term מקצת חכמינו 'some of our
sages', *Or Adonai*, p 35 b

and general good. In this way they tried to solve the
problem of injustice as well as the question of evil, how
they can be related to God. The evil is severed from the
direct connexion with God. It befalls man when forsaken
to the natural order, caused by sidereal or spherical
influence.[190]

This confused theory is justly rejected, for according
to it the main emphasis is laid upon contemplation, and
a man can be as wicked as possible, yet by virtue of his
philosophical attainments be entitled to special Providence,
which is contrary to every religious principle Again, the
undue influence of the spheres causes shrinkage in Divine
providence. Crescas, therefore, propounds his own solution.
It is actuated by a deep religious motive, but at the same
time by an exalted feeling which may compare in depth to
the Kantian theory of ethical autonomy. The real good is
not the material good, nor is the real bad the material evil,
but the spiritual. It has been evidenced by experience that
practice of virtue brings about the acquisition by the soul
of a tendency and inclination to virtue, and surely this
tendency is strengthened if it was there before. The more
a man practises virtue under adverse circumstances the
greater his perfection It follows then that when the
righteous suffer it is really for their own good, for by this
their perfection increases, and their inclination is deepened,
which is the real good.[191] Crescas does not exclude other

---

[190] *Milhamot*, IV, 6, *Or Adonai*, p. 36 a.

[191] וזה אמנם אחר שנתאמתה ההקדמה האומרת שהפעולות יקנו תכונה
ומדה קבועה בנפש וכ"ש שיחזקו אותה אם היא קנויה בכבר, ולזה יתאמת
שהמנוחה בפעל רשום בשיעמוד בנסיונו הנה כבר קנה שלמות נוסף על
שלמותו . . . . ואיך שיהיה הנה הרע שיגיע בדרך הזה ואם היה שלא
תהיה תכליתו טוב נשמי הנה הוא טוב גמור אחרי שהונח הגמול ראשיי
הוא הנפשיי, *Or Adonai*, p 37 b

possibilities such as have been put forth by previous thinkers, as evil occurring to the righteous through ancestral wrongs [102] or other causes. He, however, does not succeed with the other part of the problem, why the wicked prosper. He resorts to the usual methods employed by his predecessors. He remarks, nevertheless, that it is possible that the good of the wicked is for the purpose of spiritual badness, but it does not work out so well as in the first case

The question of the existence of evil in this world is answered by him, that there is not such a thing in the world. We must observe here that all these philosophers have never reflected upon the natural evil which abounds so much in the external world, they concentrate their discussions upon human events, and though these may arise through natural agencies, yet the question of the wherefore of such agencies of destruction has never been taken up, otherwise they would form a better conception of natural law. Maimonides makes some remarks on the subject attributing evil to the imperfection of matter, but does not treat the problem sufficiently The bad things that befall the righteous have been shown to be for the purpose of the good, and as for the sufferings of the wicked such a phenomenon from the point of justice cannot be called but good. Crescas here takes up a third question. It has been asked, How can we say that God's providence extends to man ? Is it not a belittling of God to speak of Him as being interested in man ? In answer to this,

[102] Such a solution of the question was not unknown to the ancient Greeks The whole trilogy of Oedipus Rex and Antigone by Sophocles is interwoven with that idea Oedipus and his children suffer through no wrong of their own, but because of the ancient curse on the house of Laius

Crescas brings out an interesting point in his theory. We have seen, he says, that God through His will is the cause of the existing things and their continual creation. But there is no will in regard to a certain thing unless there is a certain desire or love for the things created by that will. It follows, then, that since there is a love of God for the created things, that those things should be provided no matter what the actual causal relation is, whether mediate or immediate, for the love of God which is strictly connected with His creative will permeates them all, and there is no belittling in saying that God takes interest in man. This love of God to His created things does not lay any special emphasis upon the degree of contemplation the being possesses.[193] This remark is intended against the Jewish Peripatetics who, as remarked, made speculation an important step in the ladder of Providence. The difference between this kind of love of God, which is ethical, and that of Spinoza's, which is strictly intellectual, has been remarked above [194] The interesting Spinozistic discussion of evil, which resembles in some point that of Crescas, will be discussed with the question of determinism.

POTENCE.

Since it is evidenced by experience and reason that incapacity is a defect in God, it follows that God's potence is infinite in all respects, in whatever way reason may conceive its existence, though experience may not corroborate it. He is omnipotent, for would He be limited in one way, then beyond that boundary He would be incapable, and this is contrary to the conception we have

---

[193] *Or Adonai*, p 38 a   [194] Chapter II.

of God. When saying 'infinite in all respects', Crescas explains that he means by it the inclusion of several kinds of infinite.[195] There may be, he says, an infinite in time and an infinite in strength, and he emphasizes that God is said to be infinite in both ways. He, however, expresses himself against a blind and extreme conception of omnipotence. As it was mentioned, this infinity of potence is bounded by reason. We cannot, therefore, attribute to God the accomplishment of a logical impossibility, such as the existence of two contraries in one thing at the same time. Such a limitation is really no contradiction to the concept of omnipotent, for the ability to bring about the existence of a thing which cannot be conceived by reason is not included at all by the word potence, and therefore the lack of such potence is not a defect. Likewise, we can affirm that God cannot contradict the first axioms, המושבלות הראשונות, for their annulment would imply a concentration of the contraries and such things. He is, however, not bounded by experience; we cannot assert that God cannot do such things as are impossible according to our experience, for as long as reason can possibly conceive it, it is within His sphere of potency [196]

In connexion with his discussion on potence, Crescas makes a few remarks on Aristotle's proof of the existence of God and the conception of it. Aristotle, he says, has only proved through the eternity of movements the existence of an infinite separate force in time but not in strength. In other words, the God of Aristotle is not perfect. It is true that the force moving the sphere is

[195] ואמנם אמרנו בב״ת מבל הצדדין למה שהבב״ת לו ב׳ בחינות ממנו בב״ת בזמן וממנו בב״ת בחזק, *Or Adonai*, p. 40 b

[196] *Ibid*

eternal or infinite, but it does not follow that it can move the daily sphere in less than twenty-four hours, and it may be limited by impotency. But the right conception is, he says, that there is no relation between God and the things acted upon, for all determination arises from a certain relation, but when doing away with that relation He is necessarily omnipotent. Crescas goes on to say that the infinite potence in time and strength is not only potential but actual. The attribute of potence is indetermined, for the foundation is only will, and it is this that is meant by infinite, namely, the impossibility of being determined.[197]

In comparing the Spinozistic theory of potence with that of Crescas, we notice a striking resemblance not only in conception but also in language. Spinoza, as well as Crescas, conceives God to be omnipotent, and understands by it, at least in formal language, the same thing as Crescas, that 'He decreed things through and purely from the liberty of His will'.[198] It reminds us directly of the closing sentences of the preceding paragraph, where Crescas emphasizes the relation of potence to will and defines God's infinity to consist in the lack of determination, which is exactly what Spinoza means by the liberty of His will.[199] Spinoza also quotes in several places the fact that true things cannot become false by God's potence [200] It is true that the contents of the later (especially in the *Ethics*)

---

[197] *Or Adonai*, pp. 40 b, 41 a.

[198] 'Nos vero qui iam ostendimus omnia a decreto Dei absolute dependere, dicimus deum esse omnipotentem , at postquam intelleximus cum quaedam decrevit ex mera libertate sue voluntatis, ac deinde eum esse immutabilem,' *Cogitata Metaph* , Part II, 9

[199] *Ethics*, Proposition XVII

[200] *Cogitata Metaph* , *ibid* , p 493 , *Epistola XLIII*

Spinozistic conception of omnipotence is considerably different from that of Crescas. The impersonality of it and the mechanical interpretation are too patent to ignore, while Crescas's view is surely a personal one. Crescas has not discussed the question whether God could create another world or a better one than the present, a question which is discussed by Spinoza at great length in *scholia* to propositions XVII and XXXII in his first book of *Ethics*, and to which he gives a negative answer, but from the trend of Crescas's thought it can be inferred that he would be forced, following the logic of his reasoning, to assume a similar view. If, as he insists, God is indeterminate and infinitely perfect, what then prevented Him from creating that other world unless we should attribute to Him imperfection. But Crescas really never followed the logical conclusions to the extreme, but always turned off at an angle (as has been remarked above in Chapter II concerning the unity of God). The same occurred here, he uses his definition of infinite potence rather to prove the possibility of miracles and *creatio ex nihilo*, which really do not follow logically. We shall return to this subject once again

Free Will and Determinism.

Crescas, in discussing the very important question of free will and determinism, follows his usual method in analysing all the points *pro* and *contra*. The possible (האפשר) exists, for we observe that things have a number of causes, and some of them are cognizable, others are wanting, and it is possible that all the causes exist and possible that some do not exist, and since the causes are only possible then the things themselves are also only possible.

Again, many things are dependent on the human will, and it seems that man is master of himself, he can will them or not. Further, in the *Physics* of Aristotle, there is a classification of events, and in it are included such things as happen by chance and by accident. If there is no existence of the possible, how can we speak of chance and accident? Finally, if the possible does not exist, wherefore all the endeavour and diligence that man displays in his daily occupations, of what avail all the preparations and studies and the expenditure of energy in seeking the right way to his welfare? All these things seem so natural and common to the human nature that a denial of the possible would contradict the fundamental principle of feeling and perception.[201]

On the other side, there are many arguments against the existence of the possible. It was established in the *Physics* that all things which are corruptible come into existence only through four causes It follows then that, since their immediate causes exist, they must exist by necessity. Again, when we say that a thing is possible of existence, we mean by it that it needs a cause to over-balance the non-existent element. The existence of any possible, then, is necessitated by a preceding cause, and this cause was necessitated by another one, and so on, until we arrive at the first cause. The possible, therefore, does not exist The subject may be viewed yet from another aspect. It is accepted that whatever is being realized from the potential to the actual needs some external cause to produce it from the state of potentiality to actuality. It follows that, when the human will acts upon something, the will has changed its state from the

201 *Or Adonai*, p. 45 b.

potential to the actual. The cause of this change must
be external, such as the agreement between the desire
and the imagination which is the cause of the will.   It is
evident, therefore, that when the particular agreement
exists the will is necessitated, and if we go on searching
we shall discover causes for the arrangement, and so
further.   On the other hand, we cannot assume that the
mover of the will is the will itself, first, that would contradict the principle that a thing being realized from the
potential to the actual needs an external cause; secondly,
the will would require a preceding will as its cause, and
so on to infinity.[202]   Finally, the possible does not exist
on religious ground, for it was accepted that God's science
extends to particulars, and if events are possible it
would contradict the concept of prescience, for we can
hardly call it knowledge when the contrary to it may
occur.   It follows, then, that there exists a kind of necessity
in the order of the world.   These are the arguments
pro and *contra*[203]

Crescas, after reviewing these arguments, comes to the
conclusion that the possible exists in some aspects and in
some it does not exist.   He is, however, more inclined to
the deterministic side.   He asserts that the possible exists
only in regard to itself   In Spinozistic language it means
that when attended to itself as an isolated phenomenon
it is a possible event, but that when attended to its

[202] וכשנאמר בזה שמניע הרצון ההוא הוא הרצון לבד שהוא הפך
החיוב הנה יתחיב מזה אחד מ"ב בטולים אם שיהיה הדבר מניע לעצמו
והוא הפך ההקדמה המוסכם עליה ואם שיהיה לרצון רצון קודם יניעהו
ויוציאהו מן הבה אל הפועל ולרצון הקודם רצון אחר קודם ויתחיב רצונים
בב"ת, *Or Adonai*, p 46a

[203] *Ibid.*, p. 47 a–b.

causes and viewed in the long chain of causality the event is necessary. He proceeds then to refute the arguments produced on behalf of the possible, even in regard to its causes. The first argument saying that with some things it is possible that all their causes are found, and possible that some do not exist, is simply a *petitio principii* It is just the possibility of their causes that we seek to establish The second one that appeals to common sense and for which the fact is adduced that man wills one thing or another, partakes of the same defect, for the theory of necessity asserts that the will must have a cause, and it is one cause that makes him choose one way, and another cause that makes him choose another way, and yet will remains will without strict mechanism, for the will *per se* would probably choose either of the possibilities, but the cause pushes it in one direction; still the will itself does not feel any necessity. The other argument, appealing to everyday facts of endeavour and expenditure of energy, which testify to the existence of the possible, proves only the existence of the possible *per se*, but not in respect to the causes. Nay, even these very endeavours and exertions of energy are causes in the long chain of events that bring about the state of prosperity of the man who displays them; for the causes are not determined or fixed, but can be increased or diminished.[204]

Similarly, the theory of causal necessity does not find any objection from the religious point of view. The question of the superfluity of precepts and commandments if the events are necessitated, is answered in a manner

[204] *Or Adonai*, pp 47 b, 48 a. Crescas sums up his theory in the following words: ולזה הוא מבואר שאין בכל הטענות שמצד העיון שיחייב מציאות טבע האפשר אלא בבחינת עצמות הדברים הנמצאים ולא בבחינת סבות.

resembling the refutation of the last speculative argument.
The precepts and commandments are causes in the long
chain of events that lead up to a certain action.[205]   Reward
and punishment, however, seem to form quite an obstacle
to the theory, for is it reasonable to speak of being
punished or rewarded when there is a kind of necessity
pervading human action?   Crescas nevertheless is not
dismayed, and advances a peculiar hypothesis (we shall
find its counterpart in Spinoza).   If we look upon reward
and punishment as the effects of observing the precepts
and their transgressions there is no injustice, just as there
is no injustice in the fact that a man is scorched on
touching fire, even when that touching is accomplished
without any wilful inclination.   In short, there is a strict
cause and effect necessity which brings about that punishment should follow from one or reward from the other with
the same force as any natural phenomenon follows from
its cause.[206]

The view of Crescas on the question of determinism
and free will is already apparent though presented in an
indirect way   To sum up, events are possible *per se* but
necessary through their causes, and the one does not
conflict with the other.   The potentiality of the primal
matter, according to the Aristotelian conception, serves

[205] אבל אם הדברים אפשריים ומחויבים בבחינת סבותיהם לא יהיו
המצות והאזהרות לבטלה אבל לתכלית חשוב וזה כי יהיו סבות מניעות
לדברים אשר הם אפשריים בעצמם במדרגת הסבות, *Ibid.*

[206] ואמנם כשנתבונן בה אין התרה ממה שיקשה זה שאם היו הגמול
והעונש מתחיבים מהעבודיות והעברות (העברות perhaps) התחיב המסובבים
מן הסבות הנה לא יאמר בהם היותם עול כמי שאיננו עול הקרבות אל
האש שישרף ואם היתה קרבתו בזולת רצון, and further in the page
ולא ירגישו שהענש נמשך מהעברו בהמשך המסובב מן הסבה, *Or Adonai*,
p. 48 a.

as an excellent example for Crescas   Matter is potential
in assuming various forms in succession, but, in regard
to the causes of each form being realized, that form is
necessary especially after it was realized.   Similarly, in
human actions, each action *per se* might have occurred
or not, but in regard to the causes that brought about
its occurrence it is necessary.   However, the publication
of such a theory would be a rather dangerous weapon
in the hands of the wicked who could not see the necessary
consequences entailed by the evil acts   God, therefore,
revealed His precepts and prohibitions in order that they
should become causes and directors of human actions
towards the way leading to human happiness.   The foundation of free will (for this is not denied entirely), according
to Crescas, lies in the fact that man is ignorant of the real
situation or at least does not feel the force of the causal
chain   It is because of this that the human will and
determination become a factor in the long causal nexus.
On the other hand, when man is self-conscious that he has
done a certain act against his will, such as when a man
is compelled by external forces to commit a certain crime,
it follows that no punishment should be meted out to him,
at least by legislators, for the self-consciousness of freedom
which is a factor in the action, was absent.[207]   A similar
theory of freedom as relating to human consciousness is
advanced by Kant [208]

As for the relation of future events to prescience, we
must admit, says Crescas, that events are not possible in
regard to their being known beforehand but in regard
to themselves.   The science of God is beyond time, His

---

[207] *Or Adonai*, p 48 a–b

[208] *Metaphysical Foundations of Ethics*, p 67 and note *ad locum*

W.   K

knowledge of the future is like His knowledge of things
existing which does not impart an essential necessity to
them, for there is still some room for the possible in so far
as endeavours and attempts are factors in the decision.
But that does not affect the knowledge of God, for in
whichever way the event may result He would have known
it beforehand [209] We have seen above that this same
remark of God's science being above time was as well
as the last assertions already advanced by Saadia. The
originality in Crescas consists in his conception of the
nature of events, and in admitting only a partial kind
of freedom, an anticipation which was followed by great
philosophers.

Spinoza's view on the question of determinism resembles
that of Crescas in a good many ways, especially in its first
stage, for in his view there is to be noticed a kind of
gradation which is apparent when we compare his earlier
writings, the *Cogitata Metaphysica*, with his *Ethics*
Spinoza, more than Crescas, must, by the virtue of his
whole system, viewing things in a strictly causalistic chain,
be a determinist, yet in his early work he attempts a
reconciliation between necessity and liberty which looks
almost Crescasian, even in language. In *Cogitata Metaphysica* he says :[210] 'If we attend to our nature, we are free
in our actions and deliberate about many things for the
sole reason because we wish to. On the other hand, if
we attend to the Divine nature we perceive clearly and

[209] *Or Adonai*, p 48 b

[210] *Cogitata Metaph*, Pars I, ch 3 'Si ad nostram naturam attendamus,
nos in nostris actionibus esse liberos, et de multis deliberare propter id solum
quod volumus, si etiam ad dei naturam attendamus ut modo ostendimus clare
et distincte percipimus, omnia ab ipso pendere, nihilque existere nisi quod
ab aeterno a Deo decretum est ut existat '

distinctly that everything depends upon Him, and nothing
exists except that which was eternally decreed by God
that it should exist'. He expresses, however, his ignorance
to conceive how both necessity and liberty are compatible,
and simply says that there are many things that escape
human comprehension. Again, in the same work in the
second part, Spinoza asserts once more the liberty of man,
in spite of his taking cognizance of the causal force which
impels the mind to affirm or negate.[211] He does not explain
how the thing is accomplished, but in a previous section
Spinoza again declares his ignorance.[212] We see, therefore, that Spinoza grapples with the problem in the same
manner as Crescas does, and like him assumes that actions
are possible *per se*, and necessary through the causal chain
But we must admit that Spinoza does not carry that
principle out with the same consistency as Crescas, and
later abandons human freedom entirely, and then again
speaks in its name trying to save it at least in a shadowy
form.

Fischer insists that even in *Cogitata Metaphysica* Spinoza
is already an avowed and thorough determinist, and con-
strues his confession of ignorance in respect to the way
human liberty exists in spite of necessity to mean that
we conceive that human liberty does not exist.[213] He
quotes a number of passages to substantiate his view, but
in reality these passages do not add more to what is said
in the passage quoted where Spinoza makes his confession.
All that they show is that Spinoza recognizes the chain
of necessity, and that man is a part of nature, but this
is also contained in the passage quoted above. On the

[211] *Cogitata Metaph.*, Pars II, ch 12, p. 503
[212] *Ibid.*, ch. 11, p 500   [213] *Spinoza*, p 308.

other hand, Fischei fails to explain a fact which decidedly shows that there are two stages in Spinoza's conception of freedom. This is the famous example of Buridan's ass. In his earlier work (*Cogitata Metaphysica*) Spinoza asserts that were a man placed in such an equilibrium of forces to die of hunger, he would not be considered a man but the most stupid donkey.[214] On the other hand, in the *Ethics*, the same example is quoted, and Spinoza remarks · ' I am quite ready to admit that a man placed in the equilibrium described would die of hunger and thirst. If I am asked whether such a one should not rather be considered an ass than a man, I answer that I do not know '.[215] Spinoza agrees with Crescas in the theological question of punishment   The wicked, he says, are punished by a decree of God, and if you ask why they should be punished since they are acting from their own nature, we may reply, Why should poisonous snakes be exterminated ?[216] In his letter to Oldenburg,[217] a more striking example is given ' He who goes mad from the bite of a dog is excusable, yet he is rightly suffocated '   This is exactly the same as the saying by Crescas that whoever touches fire must be burned.

In the *Ethics*, Spinoza becomes an absolute determinist.

[214] *Cogitata Metaph* , Pars II, ch 11 'Quod autem anima tantem potentiam habeat quamvis a nullis rebus externis determinetur commodissime explicari potest exemplo asinae Buridani. Si enim hominem loco asinae ponamus in tali aequilibrio positum, homo non pro re cogitante sed pro turpissimo asino erit habendus, si fame et site pereat'

[215] *Ethics*, scholium to proposition XLIX.

[216] *Cogitata Metaph* , Pars II, ch. 8 'At respondeo etiam ex decreto divino esse ut puniatur et si tantum illi quos non nisi ex libertate fingimus peccare essent puniendi, cur homines serpentes venonosos exterminare conantur, ex natura enim propria tantum peccant nec aliud possunt'

[217] *Epist. XLI.*

Man is viewed as a part of nature subject to its laws and regulations,[218] and free will is openly denied. 'The mind is determined to wish this or that by a cause which has also been determined by another cause, and so on to infinity'.[219] Yet in spite of all this, Spinoza does not want to give up freedom, and tries to maintain it by all means. The way Spinoza reaches freedom, though different from that of Crescas who makes man's consciousness of freedom a factor in determining human action (a way which was followed by Kant, as indicated above), yet retains the basic Crescasian principle, namely, that human endeavour is a cause in the determination of human act. Spinoza arrives at the conception of freedom mainly through his principle of self-preservation   Everything in so far as it is itself endeavours to persist in its own being, says Spinoza,[220] but the principle itself would not be fruitful unless we emphasize the 'own', namely, the principle of individuality. It is true that man is a part of nature, but a higher part or at least a different part than that of the animal, and as such his essence or his nature must be different in degree from that of the animal or the stone. The persistence of man in his own being will also be different from the persistence of the animal, and this is to be called virtue according to the definition. 'Virtue in so far as it is referred to man is a man's nature or essence, in so far as it has the power of effecting what can only be understood by the laws of that nature.'[221] 'This effort for self-preservation is nothing else but the essence of the thing in question', writes Spinoza, 'which in so far as it exists such as it is,

[218] *Ethics*, IV, p 4.
[219] *Ibid*, II, 48
[220] *Ibid*, III, 1
[221] Def VIII, Book III.

is conceived to have force for continuing in existence.'[222]
It is clear from the foregoing that man does possess a kind
of determination and is not merely mechanically acted
upon. The idea of self-preservation carries in itself already
the conception of a struggle, there is something external
which tends to destroy the individual or to pervert it
from developing according to its own laws; it is against
this external force that the power of self-preservation
battles. This is well recognized by Spinoza when he says:
'The force whereby a man persists in existing is limited,
and is infinitely surpassed by the power of external
causes'[223] The term 'infinitely' may probably refer to
physical existence, but not to existence according to its
own laws, for otherwise it is impossible to conceive how
man can ever become free even in the Spinozistic fashion
Hence follows the bondage of man, which means his subjection to emotions and passions the causes of which are
external, and do not follow from the laws of his nature.

Where then is the way to freedom? This consists
simply in positing against a lower emotion which intends
to enslave the activities of man [224] another one, for an
emotion can only be controlled or destroyed by another
one contrary thereto and with more power.[225] It is here
that knowledge comes in as a potent factor, for by means
of it man can discern what is useful to him, and so perceive
his own being.[226] Ascending in the scale of knowledge,
we find that the highest point is to know God, which in
other words means to know true nature and its unfoldings,
man's own powers included. It follows then that when
man reaches that state or is on the path to it that he is

---

[222] *Ethics*, IV, 26, demon   [223] *Ibid.*, III   [224] *Ibid.*, IV, 5.
[225] *Ibid*, 6.   [226] *Ibid.*, 20.

said to be free, for viewing things under the species of reason,[227] he must necessarily follow the laws of his own nature and avoid things which tend to sway him from that or subject him to bondage. Spinoza goes on to show in detail the way man frees himself; and his ethical conception is evolved through that notion of freedom. But that does not concern us here. What we wish to show is the generation of that freedom, and what it is. To sum up, Spinoza's freedom is not a free-willist's freedom, but a reasonable intrinsic necessity, subject to immutable laws, as against a slavish irrational necessity subject to external causes the results of which tend toward destruction. This human freedom corresponds exactly to that Divine freedom of which Spinoza speaks in his first book, where the main element consists in the absence of external forces coercing it. What interests us mainly in the theory is the recognition of the struggle, and the consideration of the human power as a factor in bringing about the result, the same steps which were taken by Crescas to liberate man and restore to him a part of his lost freedom.

As regards the question of evil, Spinoza gives on that point a clear and more comprehensive explanation than that of Crescas. His view is analogous to that of the Peripatetics who saw in evil a kind of imperfection which cannot be attributed to God but to matter. Spinoza denies entirely the positive existence of evil and error,[228] for in so far as any act of evil expresses reality it is not evil, the badness of it comes only in comparison with another act of more perfection,[229] and so the whole conception of it is only human.[230]

[227] *Ethics*, IV, 67.

[229] *Epist. XIX*

[228] *Epist XXIII*, ed. Vloten

[230] *Cogitata Metaph.*, II, ch 8

To return to Crescas, he feels that the question of conciliating Divine justice with that of necessity ought to be discussed more thoroughly. He endeavoured to establish the difference between necessity without man being conscious of it, and that where the subject is conscious. It seems, nevertheless, that since reward and punishment are evolved from good and bad acts as effects from causes, there is really no reason for this distinction, for the cause is a cause just the same whether accompanied by consciousness or not. But then the whole foundation of punishment, whether Divine or human, is undermined, for both assume this distinction as their basis [231] Another difficulty is raised by the question of dogmas. Religion requires its adherents to believe in certain dogmas, but what connexion has will with dogma? Crescas produces three arguments against the possibility that will may be a necessary element in belief. First, if will is pre-requisite to belief, then belief does not possess that kind of truth which it claims to possess, for the nature of will carries the possible with it, either man wills to believe or not, and he may also will contrarily in succession; where then is the truth? Secondly, belief implies that a certain thing exists outside of the mind as well as in the mind, and if so what dependence can it have on the will, especially if a certain kind of dogma is necessitated by proofs? It is impossible not to believe it. What foundations have, then, the punitive measures attached to dogmas? [232]

In answer to these questions, Crescas reiterates his doctrine that God's precepts act as causes in determining human actions. Divine righteousness aims at the good

and the perfection of man. The precepts are instituted
by God as incitements for good actions, and the rewards
and punishments really are evolved from them as effects
from causes. But as for the question, why is consciousness
necessary in order to receive reward or punishment for the
committing of a certain act, it will be answered if we look
upon actions in the light of their intensity. The most
important ethical quality in doing good is the joy and
intensity of pleasure experienced while carrying out the
will to do good. God possesses absolute love and intensity
of doing good; the human intensity would therefore form
a link in the human relation to God. It is evident, therefore, that when this will and intensity are absent, such
as when things are committed from conscious necessity,
the actions do not entail either reward when they are good
or punishment when wrong, for there is also a kind of
intensity in doing evil as it is the love and intensity that
form important ingredients in the causing of reward and
punishment.[233]

In the same light we may solve the question of dogmas.
It is true that essentially dogmas are not related to will,
but they may be connected in some way. It is not the
belief in the dogmas that counts, but the intensity and
pleasure which a religious man feels at the believing, or in
the endeavour to follow up to the root of the matter.
This intensity and pleasure is a matter of will and choice,
for a thing may be true and man may conceive it as such

[233] ואמנם ההבדל אשר בין החיוב בזולת הרגש אונס והכרח ובין החיוב
אשר בהרגש באונס והברח הנה הוא הראוי וזה שכבר יתבאר ... במקומות
מתחלפים שהתכלי הנכסף בעבודות ופעולות הטוב הוא החשק והשמחה
בהם שאיננו דבר זולת ערבות הרצון לפעול הטוב ולזה היה ראוי שימשך
ממנו הגמול והעונש בהמשך המסובב מן הסבה, *Or Adonai*, p. 47 b.

without experiencing any particular emotion, as, for instance, the fact that the thiee angles of a triangle are equal to two right angles , but the knowledge of certain dogmas may be accompanied by the emotion if there is the corresponding exertion.   It is from this point of view that reward and punishment are attached to dogmas.[234]

[234] *Or Adonai*, p. 50 a

CHAPTER VI

TELEOLOGY AND ETHICS.

THERE are four possible ends which may be the goal of human life, (*a*) either the practical-ethical, that is, the perfection of morals, (*b*) or contemplation, or happiness, which may be (*c*) material, or (*d*) spiritual The object is, then, to determine which of these is the final end, for while all may be mediate ends, there must be a final one which is the highest of all   Crescas proceeds then to eliminate some.   Material happiness cannot be thought of as a final end in view of the fact that we posited as a possible end also spiritual happiness.   A final end must *eo ipso* be the highest , but material happiness, no matter how great, is only temporal, while spiritual, meaning the happiness of the soul, may be eternal.   It follows that the balance is on the side of soul happiness   As for the perfection of morals, though it is undoubtedly a great end, it cannot be viewed as a final end.   It is the means to purify the soul and overcome the passions that prevent the soul from reaching the desired perfection.   It also helps to bring out the latent qualities and develop the powers of the soul, and as such it is a subsidiary one   It is rather curious to hear such an opinion from Crescas, who showed himself several times endowed with a true ethical spirit,

139

and giving an autonomous basis to good deeds, to speak of morality as preparatory to development of contemplative power, the very idea which he immediately combats.[235] It may be explained that even Crescas had to pay his toll to the spirit of the age.

Crescas devotes some attention to the discussion of the perfection of thought and contemplation as a final end. Some (most likely he refers to Gersonides), he says, have developed such a theory. It is known that the mind becomes assimilated with the conceptions it perceives. In other words, the substance of the mind increases by means of the conceptions, and so we have finally an acquired mind (שכלהנקנה) which is to a certain degree different from the potential mind, or, as Aristotle called it, the passive mind.[236] Since this acquired mind is different from the potential in so far as the last is only potence, Gersonides as well as Crescas in exposition calls that hiiulian, after analogy of ὕλη, matter, potential. It is eternal in spite of being generated, for it has no cause of destruction since it does not contain anything material. Eternal happiness will therefore consist in contemplation and reason, for it is this only that gives immortality.[237] The higher the conception, the greater the degree of

[235] ואולם שלמות המדות אין בהם היות סבה עצמית בזכוך הנפש ואורה והסר ממנה תלאתה והתקרשת מטומאות מתאוות הקנאה והנצוח שהם סבות הקרובות (מקרבות והכנה לפתח perhaps) לבבי אורה אשר כל זה בה, הצעה המושכלות, *Or Adonai*, p 52a–b

[236] This idea of an acquired 'nous' was already taught by Alexander, from whom the mediaeval philosophers borrowed it   See Zeller, *Greek Philosophy*, p 296; also *Milhamot* by Gersonides, sect. 1, chs. 1, 2

[237] לזה תהיה ההצלחה הנצחית במושכלות הגקנות וכל עוד שנשיג מושגים רבים תהיה ההצלחה יותר גדולה וכל שכן כאשר יהיו המושגים יותר יקרים בעצמם, *Or Adonai*, p. 52 b; also *Milhamot*, sect. 1, chs. 7–14.

eternity and that of happiness. Even during life we experience pleasure from thinking, and so much more after death, when, freed from hindrances, the acquired reason unites with the active reason (ποιητικὸς νοῦς) and the range of conception is increased, and in the same degree also that of the intellectual pleasure   In that theory there are to be distinguished two tendencies, a more rationalistic and a religious. The first says that happiness increases with the number of ideas, of whatever character these ideas may be, whether of the physical or the spiritual world, for the active reason contains in itself the order of all existing things, and so the larger the scope of ideas the nearer the approach to the active reason on the part of the acquired.   The second emphasizes the necessity of acquiring true ideas of God and the spiritual world.

Against this theory Crescas directs his criticism   If, as the intellectualistic theory asserts, the acquired reason is a separate thing, and remains eternal while the body as well as the soul, that is the perceptive one, perishes, it is impossible that this perfection should be the end of life   Otherwise, we should have the anomalous phenomenon of a being striving for an end which is really not its own perfection, but of another being which is quite distinguished from itself.   It does not agree with reason nor with Divine justice that the reward and punishment should be meted out to a being which really has very little to do with the one who followed the precepts or transgressed them.[238]   Besides, the theory *per se* is full of contradictions, since the acquired reason is something different from the hiulian, that is the ordinary perceptive, mind, then it has no subject

[238] *Or Adonai,* p. 53 a.

out of which it is generated; it follows, then, that it is
generated out of nothing, which is contradictory to all
principles   Again, there is a contradiction in terms in the
dictum that reason acquires its essence through the conceptions   Which reason is meant here?   Shall we say
the hitulian?   But its essence is not acquired, it is given;
and the essence acquired through conceptions is something
different.   It must then be the acquired reason; but it is
impossible to speak of it as reason since it does not exist
as yet.[239]   It is evident from the foregoing that the intellectualistic theory is untenable   It remains for us to
find a *tertium quid* which shall serve as the final end
leading to spiritual happiness and eternity.   This Crescas
finds in the love of God[240]   It is not an intellectual concept
by all means, and widely different from the Peripatetic
notion as well as the Spinozistic, though the intellect may
be a useful ingredient in it.   It is best understood and
conceived after the consideration of three propositions.
First that the human soul which is the form of the body
is a spiritual being and potential in regard to conception.
The second, that the perfect being loves the good and
perfection, and that desire for it as well as its intensity
is proportional to the degree of perfection the said being
possesses   Third, that love and intensity of desire for
a thing are not related to the intellectual vigour employed
in conceiving that thing.[241]   The establishment of these
three propositions is very interesting, for the first proposi-

[239] ומהם שהמאמר הזה סותר נפשו כי כשהונח שהשכל מתעצם ממשניו
הנה אין הכוונה בו השכל ההיולני. וזה שהשכל שהתעצם כבר הונח נבדל
מה מההיולני ואם נכוין בו אל השכל הנקנה הנה אמרנו שהוא מתעצם
ברמש מושגיו כבר נבית הן נמצא קודם היותו, *Or Adonai*, p. 53 a.

[240] *Ibid.*, p. 53 b.   [241] *Ibid*, 54 a.

tion contains in a short form the psychology of Crescas,
while the other two relate to the foundation of his ethical
theory. The soul is the form of the body, for we see that
on its departure the body becomes corrupted just as do
things without form. Again, it is spiritual, for it possesses
powers which are not dependent on the senses, such as
imagination, memory, and reason. It is potential of conception or reasoning, for it is evident that it is the subject
of the reasoning power, since that one is related to the
body by means of the soul. Crescas then endeavours
to prove his statement that the soul is the subject of the
potentiality But as it is objected that since the soul
is a form it cannot be a subject, for forms are not subjects
for other forms, we must therefore suppose that this is
done through the medium of the body [242] This theory
is primarily Aristotelean in its main concepts, except that
it differs in the concept of immortality.

The second proposition treating of perfection and the love
of good is evidenced from the following : God, who is the
source and fountain of all perfection, loves the good, for this
can be seen through his causing general existence of beings
and the continual creation—here we see already the origin
of the dictum, 'reality is good', which will play an important part later—and since the causality is all through
His will, it is necessitated that the love of the good is an
essential conception of His perfection. It follows, then,
that the higher the perfection the stronger the love and
the intensity of the desire to do good, for God possesses
the highest perfection and at the same time the strongest
will to do good as evidenced from creation [243] The third

[242] It is all Aristotelean.
[243] ואם הב' תתאמת כן לפי שהוא ידוע שהשם יתברך מקור ומבוע

one, asserting that intensity of desire is independent of reasoning, is proved by definition of the terms. Will is a relation between the appetitive and the imaginative powers, and according to the degree of relation will be the intensity of the desire. Reason, on the other hand, depends on concepts and principles, both of which reside in the reasoning faculty, and that faculty is different from the imaginative and appetitive. It is evident that intensity of desire is independent of reason. After establishing these three propositions, Crescas formulates his theory of immortality and purpose, which follow as a result of the premises. Since it has been proved in the first proposition that the soul is a spiritual being, it may be immortal after its departure from the body, for it has no factors of corruption. The second proposition showed us that the love of the good is proportional to the degree of the perfection of the soul, the converse follows that the higher the good loved, the higher the perfection. It is evident, therefore, that the love of God, who is infinitely good, is necessary for the perfection of the soul. As for the independence of this love of contemplation and intellectual exercise, it was established by the third proposition.[244] It is seen, then, that the essential thing for the perfection of the soul is something independent of contemplation, and that is the love of God. Since we have seen that there is nothing lasting about man except his soul, and

מהשלמיות כלם והוא יתברך לשלמותו אשר הוא עצמותו אוהב הטוב
למה שנראה מפעולותיו בהמצאת המציאות בכלל והתמדתו וחדושות מיד
וזה אמנם ברצונו הפשוט היה בהכרח אהבת הטוב משיג עצמו לשלמותו,
Or Adonai, p 54 b.

[244] ולפי שהתבאר בג׳ שהאהבה והערבות בה זולת ההשכלה הנה העצמיי
לשלמות הנפש הוא דבר זולת ההשכלה והוא האהבה, Ibid, p. 55 a.

that the perfection of the soul consists in the love of God and the intensity of that love, it follows that this is the end and purpose of human life

In positing the love of God as an end of human life Crescas laid the foundation of a high ethical system, for the love of God is urged not on religious mystical ground as the Neo-Platonists used to speak of a longing of the soul to return to its source, but mainly because the love of God is really the love of good   The centre of ethical virtue is transferred from the mind to the heart, from the cold logical syllogisms to the warm feeling of man.   It is not the contemplative side that is emphasized, as has been done continually from Aristotle down, but the practical side.   This part, however, would not speak so much for Crescas's originality, for it simply keeps in line with the pure Jewish ethics, but what is interesting in Crescas is that he raises the ethical principle to a cosmic one, since he sees in it the basis of creation, as follows

There are two final ends; though this statement seems contradictory at first, yet it can be made consistent.   The word 'final' must be viewed under two different aspects, in respect to human life and action, and in respect to God [245]   As for the first, we have already seen what that end is.   As regards the Divine purpose, it must be the distribution of good.   The final end spoken of does not refer only to the human genus, but to the universe as a whole   There is a manifest purpose in it, in spite of the prevailing necessity of natural law, and the purpose

[245] אלא שמציאות ב' התכליות מחויבים כמו שקדם אבל בבחינות מתחלפות כי הנה בבחינת המצוה התכלית האחרון הוא האהבה ובבחינת המצוה התכלית האחרון הוא הקנאת הטוב, *Or Adonai*, p. 56 b.

W.   L

is really one in genus in regard to man and the universe.[246]

But in order to conceive this ' purpose ' clearly, a little more discussion as regards the becoming of the world is necessary   It is accepted that the universe in its manifoldness presents a certain unity and an interdependence of its parts.   This unity would lead us to accept the unity of purpose, but here a problem presents itself to us.   It is known that from the simple arises the simple, and since God is the absolute simplest being, whence then the multitude of composite beings?   The various answers proposed to that problem are insufficient.   The theory of emanations which sees in existence a gradual descending scale from pure spirituality to materiality, is inadequate, for the problem is still there. Whence the matter? Another explanation, saying that the caused beings by being caused, that is, by being possible of existence, acquire compositeness, and the lower the being in the scale of emanations the greater the compositeness, for the cause of it is also possible, since it is the third or fourth emanation, is also weak   A thing may be composite in regard to its existence, but simple in regard to essence.   Crescas offers, therefore, his solution.   It is true that if the process of causation were a mechanical one there would be no place for composition, but the fact is that it is a voluntary one. It is the will of God that is the cause of all beings, and it is through it that they arise.   But here the question arises, How can a simple being have more than one will? for in the positing of the manifold, we shall have to see

ואומר כי למה שהתבאר במה שהמציאות טוב והיה התכלית בזאת [246] התורה הקנאת הטוב . . . הנה הוא מבואר שהתכלית לכל הנמצאים ושאר התורה אחד בסוג הוא הטוב, *Or Adonai*, p. 59 b.

a manifold expression of the will. To this Crescas replies that the unity of the will consists in goodness The will to do good and distributing it is the predominant featuie[247] (the real question of will as creative cause will be discussed later in chapter VII, it is only brought in here casually). It is already manifest that the purpose in the universe is one. It is creative, not as an end to be realized, but as a cause The conception of it, according to Crescas, is best put in syllogistic form. The will of God is the will to do good Existence or reality is goodness. Hence the existing universe carries its own purpose within it.

In comparing the Spinozistic conception of the love of God (of = for) with that of Crescas, we cannot help noticing the striking similarity in form, yet there is a vast difference as to contents. There is much discussion on the subject, by those who assert that Spinoza in this impoitant teaching of his was greatly influenced by Maimonides and Crescas, his predecessors, and those who deny such influence. Of the first, the most vigorous is Joel, who ventured to go as fai as to assert that Spinoza's expression, 'The intellectual love of God', is borrowed from two sources, the 'love' from Crescas, and 'intellectual' fiom Maimonides.[248] That Joel went too fai in his assertion, and that his conclusions aie unjustifiable, is evident from a strict comparison. Howevei, a thorough investigation of the theoiy and that of Maimonides would be beyond the limits of our work, we shall, therefore, limit ourselves to Crescas

[247] זה שאם היות השכל יחייב היות לאחר הפשט רצון אחר פשוט גם בן הנה יתאמת אחדות הרצון הזה בהטבה—ולהיות כל מציאות טוב— היה להטבת האל יתברך, Or Adonai, p. 60 a

[248] Joel, Spinoza's Theologisch-Politischer Tractat, Vorwort, X.

The conception of the love of God in Spinoza forms an integral part of his system, as any of his fundamental ideas It is strictly connected with his conception of freedom, as well as with his psychology. The freedom of Spinoza, as seen,[249] is freedom from emotions, and doing such things as follow from the very essence of man and tend to self-preservation. This freedom can be obtained by inculcating in the mind a kind of controlling idea or power. But in proportion as a mental image is referred to more objects, so it is more frequent or more often vivid, and occupies the mind more [250] It follows, then, that the idea of God, which really means the comprehension of the exact order of the universe, and through which man conceives himself clearly and distinctly,[251] is such an idea which may control the mind,[252] and therefore occupy the chief place in it. This endeavour to reach the heights of understanding is termed love, for love is by definition [253] pleasure accompanied with the idea of an external cause In this conception of God we have pleasure, for pleasure is defined as a transition from lesser to greater perfection, and in conceiving the idea of God we are acquiring greater perfection, that is, more of reality and truth. Again, we conceive the causality in its fullest aspect It is also the highest virtue of the mind, for virtue in the Spinozistic conception is power or man's essence [254] This love arises only through the third kind of knowledge, or intuition,[255] namely, the possession of an adequate idea of the absolute essence of God which is eternal, for God is eternal, hence

[249] Cp. above, chapter VI

[250] *Ethics*, V, proposition XI.

[251] *Ibid*, proposition XV

[252] *Ibid*, proposition XVI

[253] Definition of Emotions, 6, II

[254] *Ethics*, III, def VIII, 4, p 28

[255] Scholium to proposition XLI, Book II, p. 32.

also the knowledge of Him, it follows also that the love which arises through it is eternal It is the quality of eternity which Spinoza connects with the love of God, that supplies a basis to the doctrine of immortality There is something eternal in the human mind, for in God there is something that expresses the essence of the body and the mind, that essence must therefore be eternal.[256] The eternity increases the more the mind conceives things under the form of eternity,[257] and this is accomplished by the knowledge of God. It follows therefore that the mind which possesses the love of God is blessed, for it attains to acquiescence of mind,[258] and perfect, since it is more of reality that it conceives, and eternal.[259] Such is Spinoza's conception of the love of God.

From the foregoing it is evident that there is very little in common between the Crescasian and the Spinozistic love of God as far as the contents are concerned, and that Joel can hardly be justified in saying that Spinoza borrowed a part of it from Crescas. The first is voluntaristic, emotional, and special emphasis is laid upon the degree and intensity of the love The second is intellectualistic and causal. Yet, as we remarked on previous occasions, in spite of their divergence there are some points of contact. Both systems have perfection for their basis. Crescas as well as Spinoza asserts that the love of God is intimately connected with perfection, and the more perfect a man is the higher the love of God, and, moreover, perfection in both systems has a background of reality. Again, according to both of them, the love of God is a means to obtain immortality, the first teaching it by a religious

[256] V, p. 23.   [257] V, p. 39.   [258] p. 28.   [259] p 39.

ethical yearning, the second by a kind of thought absorption.

Looking upon those two kinds of the love of God from an ethical point of view, namely, valuing them as ethical factors in human life, the preference ought to be given to that of Crescas. His love of God is a glowing emotional force. It is a strong desire to do good for the sake of God, for this is the way to perfection, while that of Spinoza, though serene and sublime, yet breathes cold, there is the fate of necessity hanging over it, and while it may endow a man with a brave stoicism and a kind of asceticism, yet it can hardly arouse emotions of altruism and self-sacrifice, for it is more of a negative than positive character.

That there is no purpose in nature follows from the whole system of Spinoza. He who sees everything *sub specie necessitatis* and eternal law, must perforce be a stringent antagonist of teleology. Spinoza accordingly expresses himself in his scholium to the First Book of *Ethics* deploringly of those who posit final causes in the world, or that God works for a certain end. Such a conception, according to him, is a lowering of the notion of God, and he says that it arose merely through human imagination. He is, therefore, at the first glance, wholly contradictory to Crescas, for the latter speaks of a purpose on the part of God in creating the world, yet, as has been already pointed out, the purpose of Crescas is merely an ethical one, and is not an end but a cause of beginning. As such all Spinozistic arguments against teleology fall short of it. Crescas, strengthened by the theory of purpose, makes his ethical view, the will to do good, a cosmic principle. The 'purpose' of Crescas, if examined thoroughly, amounts almost to the necessity of Spinoza, but this will be brought out in the next chapter

CHAPTER VII

DIVINE WILL AND CREATION.

CRESCAS, in basing his theory of creation, begins with a long polemical essay against those who maintain the eternity of the world, as well as against Maimonides and Gersonides, examining the physical arguments of the former, and proving the insufficiency of the defence of creation by the latter. We thought it necessary to omit all these arguments, as most of them are based on a false and antique view of nature. We shall limit ourselves to Crescas's own view, and select those points which have philosophical value.

In introducing his view, Crescas produces a general argument against those who posited the co-eternity of matter — the Peripatetics — Gentile as well as Jewish, Gersonides representing the latter. If, he says, as we have proved, God is to be conceived as the only being who is necessary of existence, it follows that all other beings, whether spiritual or material, are possible of existence and related to God as a fact to cause in some way   We cannot speak, therefore, of matter as co-existing, but as sub-existing. It is brought about by God, and it does not matter whether that bringing about is by necessity or free will   Crescas here makes a peculiar use of the term creation   He does not endeavour to prove the novelty as against the eternity of the world in the Maimonidian sense, but *creatio ex nihilo* to him means that everything was caused by God, and

outside Him nothing exists [260]   There is, however, a great
difference whether we assume the world eternal or novel,
for in the first case we assume the potence of God infinite,
in the other finite   Moreover, since God's potence is also
eternal, it follows that existence is produced by God always
and necessarily.[261]

However, existence may be caused by God in a two-fold
way, either through emanation, where the effect flows from
the cause in a natural way, or through will   Crescas
assumes that although the existence of the universe may
be necessary, yet it is not through emanation but through
will. Since we conceive God as a thinking being, it follows
that together with the bringing about of existing things
there ought to be a conception or presentation of that
existence   Again, a thinking principle wills what it desires,
we therefore conceive creation as through will.   Moreover,
the theory of emanation will always have to grapple with
the problem of the manifold and the one.   Since we have
established that God is the sole principle of existence, the
question of the existence of the composite is a menacing
one.   We must therefore have recourse to the theory of
the will.   Existence as a whole is good, and from this side
as far as it is good it is simple   It is true that viewing
it from a different angle it is manifold, but the goodness
and perfection of existence consist in the manifold being
one.   It is evident, therefore, that since reality is good and
one, God in so far as He is good must necessarily create,
hence the necessity of existence through will.[262]

[260] אבל הבונה באמרנו יש מאין הוא שנתהוה אחר ההעדר ושלא היה
לו נושא נמצא קודם, *Or Adonai*, p 69 a

[261] *Ibid*

[262] Further והיה הטוב במה שהוא טוב אחד פשוט . . . ועוד שמה מבואר

It must be admitted that Crescas has not made philo-
sophically clear how matter was created, and in what
relation it stands to God. While he combats vigorously
the co-existence of matter and makes it dependent upon
God, he does not point out in what way it was brought
about. To all difficulties arising from the manifold and
one, or the generation of matter from form he answers
that the fact that creation was through will meets the
difficulty[262] But how and in what way the will expressed
itself so as to produce a world of matter is not explained.
To one form of the problem which expresses itself in the
objection that since like produces like, how then could God
who is form produce matter which is unlike, he answers
that since existence arose through the goodness of God the
rule holds true· God is good, reality is good, so the like
produced a like result. This, however, does not answer
the question, for the difficulty how matter arose still
remains. He seems to fall back evidently on the religious
conception that God as omnipotent can do everything

A stronger relapse from his strictly logical principles into
the upholding of a religious doctrine, which is absolutely
contradictory to Crecas's whole trend of thought, is noticed
in his asserting the novelty of the world. According to his
remarks, in refuting some arguments, it follows, since God
stands in no relation to time, and all times are the same
to Him, and the more, since the world is dependent on His
will and that will is eternal, that the creation is eternal.
Yet he seems to be frightened at his own conclusions, and

בעצמו שנשלמת הטוב כשיפעל הטוב כשיפעלהו ברצון הוא יותר גדול
לאין שעור משיפעלהו בזולת רצון קוא הנהו מבואר שמהנחתינו חיוב
המציאות ממנ׳ יתחיב שיהיה על צד הרצון, *Or Adonai*, p 69a

[262] *Or Adonai*, p. 70 a.

turns around and says. 'After all, the real truth is as it is handed over in tradition, that the world was created at a certain time.' He hesitates, however, at accepting it at its surface value, and attempts to say that it is possible that there are series of worlds continually being created and destroyed, and that the novelty expressed in tradition refers only to the present world. At any rate, he does not consider it a dogma of faith. Crescas here, like all such theological thinkers, pays the price of stopping short of his own logical conclusions by being inconsistent [264]

In comparing Spinoza's view of creation with that of Crescas, we see, as usual, points of likeness and disagreement. Spinoza defines creation as an operation in which there are no other causes but the efficient one, or that created things are such to whose existence nothing is presupposed but God [265] What Spinoza intends by this definition is to exclude not only a material cause but also a final, as he himself explains in the same chapter [266] It is exactly in the same spirit that Crescas conceives creation, as has been shown. Crescas's whole tractate, though named 'Concerning the Novelty of the World', tries only to prove that the world was created *ex nihilo*, and, as has been shown, in the sense that nothing exists outside God and that matter is not co-existing. Spinoza says that he omitted the words *ex nihilo* because those who use it construe it as if the *nihil* is a subject out of which things were created.[267] In the same strain writes

[264] *Ibid*

[265] 'Creationem esse operationem in qua nullae causae praeter efficientem concurrant, sive res creata est illa quae ad existendum nihil praeter Deum praesupponit, dicimus igitur' *Cogitata Metaph*, Pars II, X

[266] *Ibid*, p 495

[267] *Ibid*, p 494 'Quin illi τó nihil non ut negationem omnes realitates consideraverunt, sed aliquid reale esse finxerunt aut imaginale fuerunt'.

Crescas, that his *ex nihilo* does not mean that *nihil* is a subject, but simply that there was no other outside subject co-existing with God. The fact that Crescas sees an end in the creation of the world, while Spinoza's definition aims to exclude it, does not destroy the similarity, for the end that Spinoza combats is an external one, but that of Crescas is in the essence of God, as has been shown, and differs but little from Spinoza's necessity according to his nature.

Spinoza, like Crescas, comes to the conclusion that the basis for an eternal world is the conception of the infinite potence of God.[268] Spinoza, in his first attempts, was not so eager to establish the eternity of the world as much as the continuity of creation, for since the will of God is eternal, creation is eternal.[269] The same thought is found in Crescas, as was shown above. Again, a similarity is also found in the conception of the will and intelligence of God as a creative power. It has been already remarked above [270] that such a similarity exists, yet to reiterate in passing, Spinoza as well as Crescas sees in creation a kind of reasonable act. In his scholium to proposition XXXII in the First Book of *Ethics*, Spinoza definitely says that God necessarily understands what He wishes, and so things could not be different from what they are, for then God's understanding ought to be different

As for the divergences, very little ought to be said, for they are patent. Spinoza's term of creation conveys an entirely different meaning from that of Crescas. It is only a convenient word, but in reality it carries with it a necessity, such a necessity as Crescas sought to escape, namely, an

[268] 'Nos illam durationem non ex sola contemplatione creatarum rerum sed ex contemplatione infinitae Dei potentiae ad creandum intellegere.'

[269] *Epist LVIII*   [270] Chapter IV

immanent one. God acts according to His nature, but whatever that nature is there is only one thing clear, that there is no room in it for voluntary actions in the usual sense. It is just this element that Crescas introduces by his voluntary creations. It is true that Crescas proves the necessity of creation by asserting that God is essentially good, and that he does not conceive of the will of God in the way that we speak of that of man's, but there is the personal element attached to it, from which Spinoza tries to escape   The fact is that the immutability of things, which forms a very important part in Spinoza's system, for it is intimately connected with his principle that things flow from God in the same way as the equality of the three angles of the triangle to two right angles, was wholly missed by Crescas. He, like Spinoza, speaks of continual creation but with an entirely different meaning, for he makes use of it to prove the possibility of miracles. Up to a certain point these two thinkers go together, but later they part company.

It is difficult to describe definitely the extent of influence an earlier thinker may exert upon a latter, especially when the latter does not name the first, but comparing the ideas expressed in *Cogitata Metaphysica*, chapter X, 'De Creatione', and those of Crescas, we find them decidedly similar, and it is a possibility that the latter took his cue from the former.

BIBLIOGRAPHY

Aaron ben Elijah   *Etz Chaym*, ed. Franz Delitzsch, Leipzig, 1841

Abraham Ibn Daud   *Ha-Emunah ha-Ramah*, Frankfurt am Main, 1852.

Aristotle   Works, ed Prantl Greek and German, Leipzig, 1854.

Baeumker, Clement   *Die Philosophie des Mittelalters*, in *Allgemeine Geschichte der Philosophie*, Berlin, 1909, quoted as *All. G. der Ph.*

Bahya ben Pekuda   *Hobot ha-Lebbabot*, ed Wilna, 1858.

Beer, T. de   *History of Philosophy in Islam*, London, 1903.

Brandis, Christian A   *Handbuch der Geschichte der Griechisch-Romischen Philosophie*, Vols I, II, Berlin, 1835.

Caird, Edward   *Evolution of Theology in Greek Philosophers*, Glasgow, 1904.

Caird, John   *Spinoza*, Edinburgh, 1888

Delitzsch, Franz   *Introduction to Etz Chaym.*

Dieterici, Friedrich H.   *Philosophie der Araber*, Vol. V, Leipzig, 1876

     ,,   ,,   *Die Theologie des Aristoteles*, Leipzig, 1882

Fisher, George Park   *History of Christian Doctrine*, New York, 1896.

Fischer, Kuno   *Geschichte der Neuern Philosophie*, Vol. II, Heidelberg, 1901

Gersonides, Levi   *Milhamot*, ed. Leipzig, 1866

Goldziher, Ignaz   *Islamische und judische Philosophie*, in *All Geschichte der Philosophie*

Grunfeld, A.   *Willensproblem in der judischen Philosophie.*

Joel, Manuel   *Don Hasdai Crescas' religionsphilosophische Lehren in ihrem geschichtlichen Einflusse dargestellt*, Breslau, 1866.

     ,,   *Zur Genesis der Lehre Spinozas*, Breslau, 1871.

Judah ha-Levi   *Kuzari*, ed Metz, Hamburg, 1838

Kaufman, David   *Geschichte der Attributenlehre in der judischen Religionsphilosophie des Mittelalters von Saadja bis Maimuni*, Gotha, 1877

Lewes, George Henry   *Aristotle, A Chapter from the History of Science*, London, 1864.

Maimonides, Moses   *More Nebuchim*, English translation, *Guide of the Perplexed*, by M. Friedländer, 3 volumes, London, 1864

     ,,   ,,   Code, Part I

     ,,   ,,   Eight chapters

Munk, Salomon   *Mélanges de Philosophie juive et arabe*, Paris, 1859

Neumark, David   *Dogmas (Ikarim Heb)*, Odessa

Saadia, Gaon   *Emunot ve Deoth*, Jusefof, 1885

Simon, Jules   *Étude de la Theodicee de Platon et Aristote*

Spinoza, Benedict   *Works*, ed Van Vloten and Land, Hague, 1882–3.

Stein, Ludwig   *Die Continuität der griechischen Philosophie in der
                      Gedankenwelt der Araber*, quoted as *C. der Gr.
                      Ph der Ar*

        ,,   *Die Willensfreiheit und ihr Verhaltniss zur gött-
                      lichen Prascienz und Providenz bei den judischen
                      Philosophen des Mittelalters*, Berlin, 1862

Taylor, Thomas   *Dissertation on the Philosophy of Aristotle*, London,
                      1812.

Wallace, Edwin   *Outlines of the Philosophy of Aristotle*, Cambridge
                      Univ. Press, 1908

Zeller, Eduard   *Greek Philosophy*, Eng trans., New York, 1890

INDEX

VITA

THE author of the book was born in the town of Slutzk, province of Minsk, Russia, in the year 1884. He received the usual Jewish education imparted to Jewish children in Hebrew schools and Talmudical academies. In 1905 he arrived in the United States, and settled in the city of New York. After preparation he entered the New York University, whence he graduated with the degree of A.B. He then took up post-graduate work in Columbia University, where he received the degree of A.M. in 1912, and was a candidate for the degree of Ph.D till 1916. Simultaneously with his study at the University he also attended the Jewish Theological Seminary at New York, whence he graduated with honors as Rabbi

Prior to the publication of this book the author published a number of essays of considerable length, the most important of which are—' Civil and Criminal Procedure of the Jewish Courts' and 'The Ethnic Character of the Jews'. He also translated into English, with introduction and notes, the famous book of Moses Hess, 'Rome and Jerusalem'.

CPSIA information can be obtained
at www.ICGtesting.com
Printed in the USA
LVHW081424200420
654120LV00012B/2067

9 780342 622825